# STAFFING THE MODERN LIBRARY

## A How-To-Do-It Manual

John M. Cohn
Ann L. Kelsey

WAGGONER LIBRARY
TREVECCA NAZARENE UNIVERSITY

*HOW-TO-DO-IT MANUALS*
*FOR LIBRARIANS*

*NUMBER 137*

NEAL-SCHUMAN PUBLISHERS, INC.
New York, London

Published by Neal-Schuman Publishers, Inc.
100 William Street
New York, NY 10038

Copyright © 2005 by John M. Cohn and Ann L. Kelsey.

All rights reserved. Reproduction of this book, in whole or in part, without written permission of the publisher is prohibited.

Printed and bound in the United States of America.

The paper used in this publication meets the minimum requirements of American National Standard for Information Sciences—Permanence of Paper for Printed Library Materials. ANSI Z39.48—1992. ∞

**Library of Congress Cataloging-in-Publication Data**

Cohn, John M.
    Staffing the modern library : a how-to-do-it manual / John M. Cohn, Ann L. Kelsey.
        p. cm. — (How-to-do-it manual series ; no. 137)
    Includes bibliographical references and index.
    ISBN: 1–55570–511–1 (alk. paper)
    1. Library personnel management. 2. Librarians—Effect of technological innovations on. 3. Library employees—Effect of technological innovations on. 4. Libraries—Automation. I. Kelsey, Ann L. II. Title. III. How-to-do-it manuals for libraries ; no. 137.

Z682.C68 2004
023.9—dc22                              2004053174

# CONTENTS

# LIST OF FIGURES

# PREFACE

Last century's revolution in electronic technology ushered in an era of extraordinarily pervasive change, one that will long continue to challenge libraries and other organizations. Affordable computers and the Internet's global linkages enable institutions to expand the nature and quality of services and offer access to formerly unavailable—even unimaginable—databases and resources. Visionary leaders respond to these changes by

- creating new positions,
- recruiting professionals with new and different skills,
- retraining existing staff, and
- contracting out library functions.

*Staffing the Modern Library: A How-To-Do-It Manual* addresses the reality that technological change often overwhelms our ability to depend entirely on in-house personnel and compels libraries to move beyond traditional jobs. Not only must we continue to overhaul job requirements, but we must also expand the very concept of staff to include workers, vendors, and service providers who perform their tasks outside the physical confines of the library. We need to forge new partnerships, collaborate with new colleagues, and build new business relationships. Staffing requires a comprehensive approach, one that recognizes and responds to continuing transformation. Today's institutions have morphed from physical spaces with defined resources into virtual enterprises with resources no longer rooted in brick and mortar.

*Staffing the Modern Library: A How-To-Do-It Manual* is organized into ten parts.

The Introduction, "Considering the Altered Environment of Libraries," establishes the foundation with an overview of how technology has (1) changed libraries, (2) affected staffing and the nature of job competencies and skills, and (3) compelled libraries to look beyond their own walls for the wherewithal to accomplish critical objectives.

Chapter 1, "Establishing a Framework: Understanding the Library as a 'Lean' Organization," bridges the gap between the structure of the literature of business management and the library to show how organizations can foster adaptability and flexibility in meeting staff needs.

Chapter 2, "Defining Twenty-first-Century Competencies: Determining Standards for the Modern Library," delineates staff skill requirements for today's library and describes how to create accurate job descriptions.

Chapter 3, "Developing Competency-based Job Descriptions: Using Reference Service as an Illustration," provides a practical example of concepts introduced in Chapters 1 and 2 using the revolution in reference service.

Chapter 4, "Facilitating the Move to Competency-based Staffing: Creating a Guide to Planning and Training," explores how these fundamental issues can make or break a smooth move to skills-based staffing solutions.

Chapter 5, "Outsourcing and Insourcing: Exploring the Options and Issues in Today's Library," examines the option of and issues related to contracting out library work.

Chapters 6, "Planning the Use of Contracted Services: Ensuring a Library's Presence on the Internet," and Chapter 7, "Arranging Other Contracted Services: Developing a Digital Collection," provide demonstrations of successfully utilizing contracted services.

Chapter 8, "Designing the Mix: Choosing What Works Best for the Library," suggests ways that libraries can determine how different approaches to staffing may be strategically employed in order to achieve the most effective results.

The Conclusion, "Broadening the Definition of 'Staff' in a Virtual World," reviews the material and proposes that the traditional meanings must be modified, given the complexities of today's electronic and virtual library environments.

At the end of this manual, you will find a "Source Guide to Staffing the Modern Library." This section presents four practical, real-world examples, including "Core and Technical Competencies for Librarians" from the New Jersey Library Association (NJLA), "Competencies for Librarians Serving Children" from Association for Library Service to Children (ALSC), "Music Librarian Competencies" from the Music Library Association (MLA), and "Sample Behavioral and Competency-based Job Description."

*Staffing the Modern Library* offers hands-on information and discussions of how present-day organizations must adopt flexible approaches to resolving workforce challenges. It includes materials on new and redefined competencies, on competency-based job descriptions, and on how libraries ought to forge innovative and productive relationships with other libraries and with organizations of all types. Worksheets and planning tools are offered throughout. Each chapter concludes with an annotated list of pertinent and practical Web-based and print resources for further information and consultation.

We hope our work will help librarians continue to imaginatively and resourcefully seek solutions to how best to staff their institutions.

# INTRODUCTION: CONSIDERING THE ALTERED ENVIRONMENT OF LIBRARIES

## HOW HAS TECHNOLOGY CHANGED THE LIBRARY ENVIRONMENT?

The traditional environment of the library was

- primarily paper-based,
- geared toward managing print resources residing within the library's walls, and
- organized around manual functions, processes, and services.

As libraries began to acquire audio and visual resources, especially during the 1960s, these newer formats were folded into the existing environment. They were managed in more or less the same fashion as paper. In the decades that followed, libraries began to introduce automated operations designed to streamline how these materials were acquired, organized, and disseminated within the library. As these processes became more sophisticated, they formed the basis of what we now call local integrated systems. This was just simply the beginning of what has become a major change in the environment of libraries.

- Print and audiovisual resources are now part of a vast array of formats accessible in libraries. Books, journals, databases in electronic format, and Web sites and home pages, as well as multimedia materials, are included in the library collections.
- Newer resources are not necessarily confined to the physical spaces of libraries. Today's library users are able to access locally, through their library or from remote locations, materials available online around the globe.
- New competitors have emerged in the information marketplace. They add value to information by changing the

way it is being collected, sorted, analyzed, and presented, and they charge accordingly.

- Libraries attempt to keep up with new formats and new technologies by seeking expertise and assistance through cooperation and collaboration with other libraries and by acquiring the services of commercial vendors.

The traditional environment for identifying, acquiring, organizing, and delivering information has become more multifaceted and complex than it ever was.

## HOW CAN WE RETHINK HOW LIBRARY FUNCTIONS ARE ACCOMPLISHED?

As the traditional paper-based library environment gave way to a new environment of print, audiovisual, multimedia, and computer-based resources, it has became necessary to reconceptualize library functions. In our book *Planning for Integrated Systems and Technologies* (Cohn, Kelsey, and Fiels 2001), we offered a model consisting of four basic functions of libraries in an electronic age (see sidebar). These four functions are not separate and distinct, but are facets of an integrated system of services provided by the modern library.

How are these functions accomplished to ensure that our users have the best possible access to information and services? Administratively, most libraries are still organized along traditional lines, with departments such as acquisitions, cataloging, circulation, reference, and serials. As the library environment changes, however, so does our need—to rethink the functions of libraries, the competencies and skills necessary to carry them out, and the importance of relying on external resources to get the work done.

There are three key issues. First, library staff in traditional positions must now be retrained in new skills sets and develop competencies that are critical to the modern library. For example:

- **Acquisitions** staff knowledgeable in obtaining books that sit on shelves must now learn how to

    - acquire *artifacts*—original objects that have an intrinsic value and that cannot be replicated in other formats;

---

**Four Basic Functions of Libraries in an Electronic Age**

1. Providing access to the content of local resources (e.g., books, periodicals, media, electronic resources) that are part of the library's collection in either hard copy or as electronic files.

2. Offering gateway or portal access to remote resources (e.g., books, periodicals, media, electronic resources), including the ability to obtain copies in print and electronic formats.

3. Facilitating off-site electronic access to local and remote resources from users' homes, offices, and schools.

4. Providing access to human assistance in locating information.

- purchase full-text electronic journals and other "published" materials that are acquired virtually, not physically;
- negotiate for access to electronic databases and other resources that the library acquires rights to but does not really own.

- **Catalogers** proficient in the intricacies of the MARC 21 standard must organize information that is often new to libraries by

  - describing digitized content that must then be controlled bibliographically and made available on local servers or through the Web;
  - learning and understanding Dublin Core *metadata* vocabulary designed to describe not only digital and Web-based resources, but any resource regardless of format or medium;
  - creating links and "hooks" to both internally held and external resources of all kinds.

- **Reference** and **instruction** librarians accustomed to face-to-face interviews or classroom-style bibliographic instruction must now interact with users who

  - are not on-site or who require service after the library is closed;
  - want to be able to submit questions and resolve problems using electronic mail, the Web, or fax transmission;
  - are engaged in some form of instruction using new communications methodologies into which the library instructional component must fit.

Second, libraries must determine how best to integrate entirely new tasks—whole jobs—that the changing environment has generated and that are not necessarily performed by traditional library staff. For example:

- **Systems managers,** who oversee massive investments in new communication and computer technologies
- **Information brokers,** who search large and complex databases on behalf of information-seeking clientele
- **Webmasters,** who ensure that libraries and their resources and services have a presence on the World Wide Web

Third, libraries must learn to reach beyond their own staff, increase their use of contract services and partnerships with other libraries and organizations to accomplish library functions, and view these arrangements as intrinsic to the library's staffing.

## HOW DO WE ENHANCE AND EXPAND STAFF RESOURCES IN A COMPLEX ENVIRONMENT?

Chapter 1 presents a theoretical framework for the rest of this book. It discusses ideas presented in a work entitled *Alliances, Outsourcing, and the Lean Organization* (Milgate 2001). Although not concerned with libraries per se, the book's premises for organizational effectiveness speak to the issues facing libraries and librarians today. These are the issues the present book will address.

The chapters that follow will focus on the development, by existing library staff, of new competencies and skills, and on the issues involved in contracting or partnering with external organizations for resources and services. Traditional—and not so traditional—functions in the modern library will be used as illustrations in each chapter, along with new job competencies and descriptions, examples of contractual agreements with outside organizations, and worksheets for use in deciding what strategies work best in meeting the challenges of technology, heightened user expectations, and change.

The library's primary goal is managing the increasingly complex web of resources, services, and relationships that ensure the effective flow of information to the library's end-user clientele. By developing a mix of approaches and solutions to developing internal competencies and building external relationships, libraries are becoming more complex but also more effective organizations. By developing a "fusion" of solutions, we are expanding our understanding of what it means to staff the contemporary, electronic library.

## SOURCES

Braun, Linda W. "New Roles: A Librarian by Any Name." Freehold, NJ: Central Jersey Regional Library Cooperative (February 1, 2002). Available: www.becomealibrarian.org/NewRoles.htm.

Originally published by *Library Journal* (Available: http://libraryjournal.reviewsnews.com/index.asp?layout=articlePrint&articleID=CA191647), this article discusses new jobs, titles, and organizational structures in libraries and takes a brief look at the outsourcing option as well.

Cohn, John, Ann L. Kelsey, and Keith Michael Fiels. 2001. *Planning for Integrated Systems and Technologies: A How-To-Do-It Manual for Librarians*. New York: Neal-Schuman.

The thrust of this book is planning for automated, integrated systems in libraries. A redefinition of library functions in the electronic age is offered in Chapter 2 as the basis for gathering and organizing data, setting priorities, and developing a technology plan.

Crouch, Marilyn. "Staffing in Public Libraries to Serve the 21st Century." Perspective Paper No. 12. Sacramento: California State Library Convocation on Providing Public Library Service to California's Twenty-first-Century Population (July 1997). Available: www.library.ca.gov/LDS/convo/convoc16.html.

The author briefly considers a number of issues confronting public library staffing in the new century, including the impact of technology, outsourcing, contracting for specialized skills, and developing new competencies in the workforce.

Deegan, Marilyn, and Simon Tanner. 2002. *Digital Futures: Strategies for the Information Age*. New York: Neal-Schuman.

This book discusses library services in the context of digitization and electronic resource development. Chapter 9 focuses on "Digital Librarians: New Roles for the Information Age," reviewing key skills, training, education, and the meaning of librarianship in a digital future.

Feather, John. 2000. *The Information Society: A Study of Continuity and Change*. 3rd edition. London: Library Association Publishing.

This book offers a broad-based look at the various dimensions of today's "information society"—historical, technological, economic, and political—focusing on changes taking place in the information marketplace, public policy concerns, and, most important for us, the changing nature of the information profession.

Milgate, Michael. 2001. *Alliances, Outsourcing, and the Lean Organization*. Westport, CT: Quorum Books.

(See Chapter 1 Sources for annotation.)

Roitberg, Nurit. "The Influence of the Electronic Library on Library Management: A Technological University Library Experience." The Hague: IFLA (May 12, 2000). Available: www.ifla.org/IV/ifla66/papers/050-132e.htm.

In this paper presented at the 66th International Federation of Library Associations General Conference, August 13–18, 2000, in Jerusalem, Israel, the author discusses the phenomenon of the electronic library developing in parallel fashion to the traditional library, requiring constant re-examination of workflow and job duties. Although the author's focus is on a technological university and research institution located in Haifa, Israel, the principles discussed apply to all types of libraries today.

Troll, Denise A. "How and Why Are Libraries Changing?" Washington, DC: Digital Library Federation (June 26, 2001). Available: www.diglib.org/use/whitepaperpv.htm.

"The purpose of this paper is . . . to explore how and why libraries and library use are changing." The focus is on academic libraries and includes some insightful material on the changing environment of libraries and user expectations.

Youngman, Daryl C. "Library Staffing Considerations in the Age of Technology: Basic Elements for Managing Change." Chicago: American Library Association, Association of College and Research Libraries, Science and Technology Section (Fall 1999). Available: www.istl.org/99-fall/article5.html.

In this article, published in the online edition of *Issues in Science and Technology Librarianship*, the author proposes a model for supporting electronic services while maintaining traditional services that incorporates three basic elements: utilization of experienced librarians with a historical perspective and mentoring skills, targeted recruiting of entry-level librarians with new skill sets, and creative supervisory practices that balance traditional roles with changing staff responsibilities.

# 1

# ESTABLISHING A FRAMEWORK: UNDERSTANDING THE LIBRARY AS A "LEAN" ORGANIZATION

## WHAT IS A "LEAN" ORGANIZATION?

*Alliances, Outsourcing, and the Lean Organization* (Milgate 2001) is part of the vast and growing literature on business management and corporate survival in a rapidly changing global environment. While it addresses issues involving public organizations to a limited degree, the book does not mention libraries at all. Still, the author's concepts offer a valuable context for the present volume and allow us to establish a base from which to discuss what we have referred to as a mix of solutions for managing library functions and sustaining the modern library.

For Milgate, organizations survive and prosper by being "lean." Lean does not mean shrinking or in decline. Rather, it means flexible, adaptable, and resourceful in meeting needs.

Milgate identifies six "building blocks" that contribute to an organization's being able to adapt and thrive:

- Core competencies
- Strategic alliances
- Effective strategic outsourcing
- New management disciplines
- Partnership culture
- Technological enablers

In summary:

- ***CORE COMPETENCIES*** are the skills, strengths, and technologies that constitute the "collective learning" of the organization. They are enduring characteristics, the glue that binds the organization into a functioning whole and allows it to succeed. They represent the organization's competitive edge.

- *STRATEGIC ALLIANCES* enable the organization to provide extra leverage for its core competencies, develop new service capabilities, or offer programs that it could not do on its own. No longer peripheral to the organization's success, they are often central to its ability to accomplish its goals, providing access to critical management skills, technologies, and other resources.

- *EFFECTIVE STRATEGIC OUTSOURCING* means contracting to have your "non-core" activities carried out by others outside your own organization. Motivating factors include reducing overhead costs, leveraging the competencies that *other* organizations have, and, of course, focusing on your own organization's interests or strengths.

- *NEW MANAGEMENT DISCIPLINES* refers to developing new skills for managing the multiple relationships—the internal teams, external alliances, outsourcing partners—that are created by the other building blocks.

- *PARTNERSHIP CULTURE* means the organization must develop a structure and internal culture that promotes external relationships and partnerships in getting the work done and accomplishing objectives.

- *TECHNOLOGY ENABLERS* means using information technology capabilities in new and creative ways, for example for training or other organizational "learning" experiences, or to enhance relationships with other organizations.

Again, Milgate's book and its conceptual framework are directed toward the corporate and industrial environments. Nonetheless, the concepts presented are pertinent to the premises of this book and help us to understand the issues we raise.

## WHAT ARE THE BUILDING BLOCKS OF THE LEAN LIBRARY ORGANIZATION?

Using Milgate's building blocks, **core competencies** represent the library's "collective learning"—the expertise, talent, and proficiencies that move the institution forward in achieving its mission. These are not immutable, however. Indeed, part of being a lean organization is to recognize when and how such competencies need to be redefined—and people retrained—so that the organization is able to meet its goals.

Most libraries understand and participate in **strategic alliances** of all kinds. A few examples are offered in Figure 1-1. They represent the realization that single institutions can no longer go it alone. Instead, they must actively pursue the benefits resulting from cooperative and collaborative efforts with other organizations. While issues of retaining autonomy, uniqueness, and local policies remain strong, most libraries accept the basic premise of forming alliances, that is, that alliances enable libraries to leverage the strengths of the many for the benefit of each participant.

**Outsourcing** is also not new to libraries. Some traditional examples of outsourcing include

- contracting for the cataloging and/or processing of new acquisitions;
- contracting for retrospective conversion services;
- contracting for binding and preserving existing parts of the collection;
- acquiring graphical or public relations services from an outside firm.

Milgate, however refers to *strategic* outsourcing. This suggests that, like forming *strategic* alliances, the decision to outsource must be made on the basis of decision making that takes into account the fundamental goals and objectives of the institution as well as the strengths and constraints of the institution's present and future environment.

Although outsourcing—or, more broadly, the contracting out of services—is often considered acceptable for "non-core" functions, it is our

---

- Joining a multitype, single, or other kind of library cooperative or network of libraries.
- Joining with another library or libraries to share a local, integrated system.
- Participating in a cooperative database purchasing arrangement with other libraries.
- Contracting with another library to share physical space (joint-use facility) or to cooperatively offer a program or service.
- Developing collaborative agreements for sharing resources (human and/or material) to accomplish an objective, such as the digitization of a specialized print collection.

**Figure 1-1. Examples of Strategic Alliances**

view that contracting for services is applicable to the broad spectrum of roles and concerns that are characteristic of the modern library, not just to marginal or peripheral tasks. Indeed, resting at the library's *core* is what it shares with all other libraries, namely, "to enable users to gain access to and use the information that they need" (Brophy 2001).

**Management discipline** entails overseeing the whole complex array of skills and relationships that move an organization forward. In a library context, this refers, for example, to

- providing the proper scope and depth of training for library staff;
- ensuring that an outsourced contract is properly fulfilled by the vendor;
- determining that services provided by a library consortium adequately fills the library's needs;
- properly evaluating the work done by "insourced" staff on a project within the library itself.

**Enabling technologies** will assist the library in effecting the changes demanded by the new service environment. For example:

- New applications for training and development can make the difference between a successful or less successful training effort.
- New telecommunications methodologies, properly used, can facilitate ongoing communications with outside parties.
- Data and budget management applications can make the job of financial control over the library's complex work arrangements more reliable and effective.

The development of a **partnership culture** will sustain over time this method of managing the library's work and ensure that a multifaceted approach will continue to characterize the library's response to ongoing change. We have all heard or read about the "culture" of an organization and how difficult it is to change it. Libraries, however, are already a long way down the road to replacing traditional forms of insularity with an acceptance of cooperation and mutual assistance. Developing new means for getting the work done will further strengthen this trend and promote a partnership, or partnering, culture in our twenty-first-century libraries.

Finally, Milgate quotes an earlier work (Prahalad and Hamel 1990, 82) in observing that "how to coordinate diverse production skills and integrate multiple technologies" (Milgate 2001, 5) is perhaps the most important core competency that constitutes an organization's collective learning. Enlarging on this view, perhaps the most important core competency for libraries today is how to sustain the effective mix of in-house competencies and skills and contracted services in order to enable the modern library to accomplish its mission. This will be the concern of the chapters to follow.

# SOURCES

Brophy, Peter. 2001. *The Library in the Twenty-first Century: New Services for the Information Age*. London: Library Association Publishing.

In Chapter 7, "The Core Functions of a Library," the author focuses on the "common mission . . . represented in all types of libraries . . . whether they are traditional or digital or hybrid services." His purpose is "to form the basis of further discussion of what the process of achieving such a mission will entail in the future."

What is notable about Brophy's approach is that he cuts across all kinds of libraries in elaborating on what he perceives to be a commonality of mission, function, and processes. However, he advocates a broad definition of the term *information* and is careful to distinguish among differences in emphasis and content as well as alternative types of "users" in our libraries.

Milgate, Michael. 2001. *Alliances, Outsourcing, and the Lean Organization*. Westport, CT: Quorum Books.

We have tried to capture the essence of Milgate's central thesis—that the "big business winners in the new millennium will be those organizations that focus most successfully on their core competencies and leverage them through a range of strategic alliances and outsourcing to create a *best of everything* network" (Milgate 2001, 1). We have modified his understanding of core competencies slightly to deal with the distinction between competencies and functions, which can be confusing because they are often intertwined.

Readers may wish to begin with a detailed and critical review of Milgate's book written by Jeffrey A. Mello in the *Journal of Organizational Change Management* 15, no. 2 (2002): 327–30. The reviewer writes that Milgate's book "breaks new ground and pushes the frontiers of management theory and practice forward . . . (with) a fresh and innovative perspective on the subject."

Prahalad, C. K., and G. Hamel. 1990. "The Core Competence of the Organization." *Harvard Business Review* 68, no. 3: 79–91.

This article is quoted by Milgate in defining and discussing his concept of core competencies.

Wilding, Tom. 2001. "External Partnerships and Academic Libraries." *Library Management* 23, no. 4/5 (August): 199–202.

Based on a paper delivered at the International Federation of Library Associations conference in Boston, Massachusetts, in 2001, this paper explores relationships between academic libraries and organizations "that extend well beyond the boundaries of the academic campus."

Woodsworth, Anne, and James F. Williams II. 1993. *Managing the Economics of Owning, Leasing, and Contracting Out Information Services*. Brookfield, VT: Ashgate.

This book's purpose is to analyze how information services are provided within libraries and information centers and describes the important factors that must be considered in making decisions about alternative methods, such as leasing staff and outsourcing. The book describes pros and cons of each method and offers advice to decision-makers on issues such as doing a cost-benefit analysis.

# 2  DEFINING TWENTY-FIRST CENTURY COMPETENCIES: DETERMINING STANDARDS FOR THE MODERN LIBRARY

## HOW ARE LIBRARY COMPETENCIES CHANGING?

Sandra Nelson and her coauthors said it plainly: "Without staff there could be no library." Further, "staff members are a resource, just like the collection" (Nelson 2000, 30). But, like collections, staff skills must be kept up-to-date if the library is to meet its goals and objectives.

The electronic era has turned this common-sense reasoning into a major challenge. As we suggested in the Introduction, we need to view the library in a different light if we are to grasp the nature of the changes that are occurring. Deegan and Tanner, cited in the Introduction, put it this way:

> Library management culture tends to focus on functions and processes rather than goals and results. There is a need to think outside of the fixed boundaries of the functional entities and hierarchies seen in most libraries to focus on the core goals and achieve them through the innovative use of the large skills base resident, but largely not optimized, in the majority of library staff. (Deegan and Tanner 2002, 228)

What this means is that we need to think differently about the competencies libraries need, the skill sets staff members must bring to bear in getting the job done, and the methods employed to train people and develop those skills. That is the focus of this chapter and the two that follow.

A word about semantics: *Competency* may be thought of as another word for *skill.* However, with the total quality management movement that

---

**Competency:** The knowledge, skills, attitudes, and values required for successful performance in a job. The demonstration of a competency includes the factors of observation, measurement, training, and learning.

**Core competency:** The skills, behaviors, and personal characteristics that all employees are expected to demonstrate. Core competencies are based on the values of the organization.

**Personal competency:** The set of competencies that an individual possesses.

**Role:** A generic set of work activities that relates to one or more specific jobs.

**Skill:** The demonstration of a particular talent such as a technical skill needed for the operation of a computer or a verbal skill needed for making a presentation.

**Figure 2-1. Some Definitions Related to Competencies**

---

began in the for-profit sector and eventually spread to public-service organizations, the expression "competency-based assessment" took hold. This implied that competencies were clearly observable outcomes that could be measured and improved through proper training, suggesting a broader range of measurable factors.

The definitions in Figure 2-1, selected and adapted from Bryant and Poustie (2001), demonstrate some of the differences among the terms that we are using in this book.

# WHY IS DEFINING COMPETENCIES IMPORTANT?

Developing a list of competencies is important for libraries because doing so

- enables the library to ensure that the organizational mission is reflected in the skills that are acquired or developed in new and existing staff;
- helps to blur the distinctions between and among traditional functions and processes that may no longer be pertinent in a changing information environment;

- assists the library in staying responsive to the changing needs and expectations of its customers and clientele;
- helps staff to understand what is expected of them;
- establishes a base line for assessment and defining development needs;
- guides management and staff in creating a program of professional and continuing education;
- helps to define what to look for among applicants during the recruitment and hiring process.

# WHAT COMPETENCIES DO LIBRARIES NEED TODAY?

What has changed most for libraries is that staff members cannot succeed simply by being task-oriented. Being skilled at tasks associated with traditional library functions is not sufficient in an environment in which change, driven so heavily by technology, alters so quickly the tasks and functions that staff members are expected to perform.

Competencies may be defined and delineated in many different ways. The Tampa Bay Library Consortium (2002) distinguishes among four types of competencies:

- **Philosophical Competencies**—understanding the library's mission, intra- and interdepartmental relationships, and relationship to other libraries and the community, as well as professional ethics and values of the library and the profession.
- **Technical Competencies**—demonstrating basic skills in the use of computer, multimedia, and information retrieval tools, as well as understanding the role of the library in promoting the use of technology.
- **Professional Competencies**—seeking out continuing education opportunities, understanding the organization and scope of resources held by the library, and communicating and collaborating effectively, as well as serving as an advocate of the library inside and outside the organization.
- **Personal Competencies**—demonstrating commitment to the profession and to good service; being self-motivated,

flexible, communicative, and positive; and using good judgment in solving problems and managing resources.

In Figure 2-2 and Figure 2-3, for the sake of comparison, we present three additional perspectives on what modern libraries need in the way of competencies. Figure 2-2 includes McNeil and Giesecke's (2001) set of twelve core competencies with a brief explanation of each. Figure 2-3 provides two additional ways of characterizing competencies:

- the approach taken by the City of Toronto, Canada—as used by the Toronto Public Library and presented in

| Competency | Description |
|---|---|
| Analytical skills/problem solving/decision making | Uses logical reasoning and sound judgment to assess situations and make decisions |
| Communication skills | Listens carefully, transmits information accurately, and seeks constructive feedback |
| Creativity/innovation | Looks for ways to apply new ideas, methods, and techniques |
| Expertise and technical knowledge | Demonstrates understanding of and ability to use up-to-date knowledge and new technology |
| Flexibility/adaptability | Responds to changes in direction and priority and accepts new challenges |
| Interpersonal/group skills | Works effectively with others across organizational and functional lines to achieve results |
| Leadership | Sets high standards and earns the respect of others through coaching and mentoring |
| Organizational understanding and global thinking | Demonstrates an understanding of the "big picture," i.e., how the institution in its entirety works |
| Ownership / accountability / dependability | Accepts responsibility for getting the job done |
| Planning and organizational skills | Anticipates changes and trends in order to allocate resources effectively and implement appropriate initiatives |
| Resource management | Demonstrates a consistent focus on minimizing expenses and maximizing results |
| Service attitude/user satisfaction | Understands and meets the needs of users |

**Figure 2-2. A List of Twelve Core Competencies and What They Mean**

Bryant and Poustie (2001)—which involves a longer list of competencies, within which five are considered core

• Henczel's (2002) professional and personal competencies for special librarians that, in her article, she matches with a separate list of "business competencies"

---

**City of Toronto/Toronto Public Library (*Bryant and Poustie 2001*)**

Adaptability

Commitment to continuous learning

Conceptual thinking

**Customer service orientation\***

Developing others

**Fiscal responsibility\***

Holding people accountable

Impact and influence

**Innovation\***

Leadership

Leading change

Listening, understanding, and responding

Organizational awareness

Planning, organizing, and coordinating

Problem solving

Relationship building

Responsiveness to the public

**Results orientation\***

Strategic orientation

Striving for clarity and quality

**Teamwork\***

(**\*Core Competencies**)

**Figure 2-3. Library Competencies: Two Additional Approaches**

**Special Libraries Association (*Henczel 2002*)**

**Professional Competencies:**

- Expert knowledge of content of information resources
- Specialized subject knowledge
- Develops / manages information services aligned with strategic directions of the organization
- Provides excellent instruction and support for users
- Designs and markets value-added information services and products
- Uses appropriate information technology
- Uses appropriate business approaches to communicating importance of information services to senior management
- Develops specialized information products for use inside and outside the organization
- Evaluates outcome of information use and conducts research on solving information management problems
- Continually improves information services in response to changing needs
- Is effective member of senior management team and consultant on information issues

**Personal Competencies:**

- Committed to service excellence
- Seeks out new challenges and opportunities
- Sees the big picture
- Looks for partnerships and alliances
- Creates an environment of mutual respect and trust
- Communicates effectively
- Works well with others in a team
- Provides leadership
- Plans, prioritizes, and focuses on what is critical
- Is committed to lifelong learning and personal career planning
- Has personal and business skills and creates new opportunities
- Recognizes the value of professional networking and solidarity
- Flexible and positive in a time of continuing change

**Figure 2-3. Library Competencies: Two Additional Approaches** (*Continued*)

The Source Guide at the end of this book offers additional examples of competencies for the modern librarian. Source A is the position of a state professional organization, the New Jersey Library Association (NJLA), on "Core Competencies for Librarians." Sources B and C offer core competencies for two very different types of library professionals: a children's librarian and a music librarian.

# WHAT ARE BASIC ELEMENTS OF COMPETENCY-BASED JOB DESCRIPTIONS?

Job descriptions are the important tools libraries and most organizations use for defining and describing titles and positions. Hence, job descriptions are where the change to a competency-based approach will manifest itself.

However they are created—whether by a board, a human resources department, library management, local government, or civil service—all job descriptions tend to have certain elements in common. These include

- the job's title
- its position within the organization
- a unique number or numbers assigned to the position
- the job description's approval date
- the position's purpose
- its duties and responsibilities
- the qualifications required for the position, including education, skills, abilities, and knowledge
- supervisory information: who supervises whom

Purpose, duties and responsibilities, and qualifications—education, skills, abilities, and knowledge—along with the job's relationship to the library's mission, are the areas most affected by the library's changing environment. They reflect most clearly the shifts from specific task-oriented approaches to the broader, enduring characteristics discussed and shown in Figures 2-1 and 2-2. In essence, the traditional task-oriented job description will focus on specific activities or actions. Competency-based job descriptions will focus on the knowledge and behaviors that are required for success.

Source D, "Sample Behavioral and Competency-based Job Description," illustrates the concept. Although it is for a position other than that of librarian, it is presented here for its comprehensive nature. Under "Qualifications" are a series of abilities and personal characteristics grouped under four broadly defined categories:

- *Experience, education, and licensure*
    - for example, "an experienced leader and financial executive"; "a strategic visionary"; "a well-organized and self-directed individual"
- *Language skills*
    - for example, "ability to respond effectively"; "ability to make effective and persuasive speeches and presentations"
- *Mathematical skills*
    - for example, "ability to apply advanced mathematical concepts"
- *Reasoning ability*
    - for example, "ability to apply principles of logical or scientific thinking"; "ability to deal with nonverbal symbolism"

Under "Essential Duties and Responsibilities" are competencies that generally emphasize outcomes over tasks. Here are some examples from the job description:

- *"Develop credibility for the finance group by providing timely and accurate analysis of budgets and financial reports that will assist the President, Board and other senior managers in managing their responsibilities;*
- *Establish credibility throughout the organization and with the Board as an effective problem solver; be viewed as approachable and a mentor to people in financial issues;*
- *Provide strategic financial input and leadership on decision-making issues affecting the organization."*

# HOW DO WE TRANSITION FROM COMPETENCIES TO SKILLS?

The terms and phrases used in the figures and illustrations in this chapter represent broad competencies that, to use a phrase from Chapter 1, represent "enduring characteristics, the glue that binds the organization into a functioning whole and allows it to succeed." Within and alongside each of these will be the need to possess or develop specific abilities and skills that will change over time as needs shift. For example, for a library moving into the development of digital content, staff members must exhibit broad competencies related to coping with technological change, developing partnerships, and managing workflows. They must, however, also be able to apply specific skills sets that include, as Tennant (1999) has described,

- the ability to capture images of physical items, such as books, journal articles, manuscripts, and photographs, as well as other kinds of objects;
- an understanding of how to manipulate text-scanning software to maximize scanning effectiveness in order to improve searching and editing;
- a knowledge of mark-up languages, such as HTML for Web pages and SGML and XML for documents and database records;
- an understanding of how metadata description captures the elements of digital images to make them coherent and useable;
- an appreciation for both simple indexing and more complex relational and object-oriented database systems;
- the ability to write specifications for an effective interface design that rests between the library's digital content and the user;
- some knowledge of programming languages such as Perl; and
- Web-development tools such as HTML codes and CGI programming.

In Chapter 3, to illustrate what we have discussed up to this point, we will take a closer look at specific competencies and job descriptions for reference librarians in the modern library. In Chapter 4, we present an overview of the planning issues that must be taken into consideration when implementing training efforts that seek to ensure the development of necessary skills among library workers and the "retooling" of experienced staff.

# SOURCES

Beck, Maureen A. 2002. "Technology Competencies in the Continuous Quality Improvement Environment: A Framework for Appraising the Performance of Library Public Services Staff." *Library Administration and Management* 16, no. 2 (Spring): 69–72.
This article discusses the employment of a competency-based model for identifying information technology skills and describes how they may be employed in the performance appraisal process.

Bryant, Josephine, and Kay Poustie. "Competencies Needed by Public Library Staff." Gutersloh, Germany: Bertelsmann Foundation (2001). Available: www.public-libraries.net/html/x_media/pdf/competencies.pdf.
This paper reviews the development and implementation of personal and technical competencies, required by library staff, in the context of the Toronto Public Library experience. Technical competencies are assessed in relation to the levels of competency among public library staff in Scotland, Finland, Canada, and Australia. A comprehensive bibliography on competencies is offered.

"Core Competencies in the Library Profession: Selected Writings." Ottawa: Art Libraries Society of North America Professional Development Committee (February 17, 2004). Available: www.uflib.ufl.edu/afa/pdc/BIBLIOGRAPHY_CORECOMPS.pdf.
This is an unannotated list originally prepared by Heather Ball for William Harvey Fisher. 2001. "Core Competencies for the Acquisitions Librarian: Analysis of Position Announcements." *Library Collections, Acquisitions, and Technical Services* 25, no. 2 (Summer): 179–90.

Deegan, Marilyn, and Simon Tanner. 2002. *Digital Futures: Strategies for the Information Age.* New York: Neal-Schuman.
This book discusses library services in the context of digitization and electronic resource development. Chapter 9 focuses on "Digital Librarians: New Roles for the Information Age," reviewing key skills, training, education, and the meaning of librarianship in a digital future.

Henczel, Sue. "Competencies for the 21st Century Information Professional: Translating the SLA Competencies into Business Competencies." Alexandria, VA: Special Libraries Association (2002). Available: www.sla.org/documents/conf/Competencies_for_the_21st.doc.
"This paper examines how the [Special Libraries Association] competencies can be mapped to the broader business competencies of marketing (promoting), packaging (product development), persuading and performing (sales/customer service) and positioning

(strategic maneuvering). It introduces a process whereby the skills, knowledge, understandings and attitudes associated with each competency are identified and matched with the skills required in a business environment."

McNeil, Beth, and Joan Giesecke. 2001. "Core Competencies for Libraries and Library Staff." In *Staff Development: A Practical Guide*, ed. Elizabeth Fuseler Avery et al., 49–62. 3rd ed. Chicago: American Library Association.

This is chapter 10 of the volume. The authors discuss the background and development of core competencies in libraries, providing the list that is the basis of one used in the present volume and offering sample interview questions "to help determine competency development or the potential for development."

Morrison, Don A., ed. 2002–2004. *Model Job Descriptions for Library Systems.* University Place, WA: Local Government Institute.

This manual, with accompanying CDs of model job descriptions and competency levels in Word document format, includes a detailed guide to writing job descriptions based on concepts discussed in Morrison's *Core Competencies for Library Systems.* The job description files cover an array of titles from the generic (e.g., Librarian I) to the very specific (e.g., Web Services Librarian). For a fuller description and list of jobs covered, see www.lgi.org/Publications/JD-LS.htm.

Nelson, Sandra, et al. 2000. *Managing for Results: Effective Resource Allocation for Public Libraries.* Chicago: American Library Association (ALA).

Chapter 2 on "Managing Your Library's Staff" is "intended to help managers determine the staffing required and identify the abilities needed to accomplish the library's service goals, objectives, and abilities." A workform based on a companion volume, *Planning for Results: A Public Library Transformation Process* (ALA 1998), is employed. See also the updated volume by Sandra Nelson, *The New Planning for Results: A Streamlined Approach* (ALA 2001), which "outlines a tested, results-driven planning process, revamped and streamlined to enable librarians to respond quickly to rapidly changing environments."

"Ohio Library Job Descriptions." Columbus: State Library of Ohio (January 2005). Available: http://winslo.state.oh.us/publib/job.html.

This Web page provides a number of sample job descriptions from public libraries, many of which are written in a competency-based format. There is also an excellent summary of the components of a competency-based job description, as well as links to other job description Web sites.

Olson, Anna. "Equity of Access Pathfinders: Equity of Access: Competencies for Librarians." Austin: University of Texas at Austin School of Information (December 2003). Available: www.ischool.utexas.edu/~access/competencies.htm.

This pathfinder, offered by the University of Texas at Austin, provides annotated links to sites that deal with the issue of competencies within the different subfields and types of libraries in the profession.

Tampa Bay Library Consortium (TBLC), Tampa, FL. "Core Competencies" (January 2004). Available: http://snoopy.tblc.lib. fl.us/training/competencies.shtml.

This section is part of the "Staff Training" page on the Consortium's Web site, which also includes material on training opportunities available through TBLC.

Tennant, Roy. 1999. "Skills for the New Millennium." *Library Journal* 124, no. 1 (January 1): 39.

This is a brief *Library Journal (LJ)* column in which essential skills for digital librarians are listed and described.

# DEVELOPING COMPETENCY-BASED JOB DESCRIPTIONS: USING REFERENCE SERVICE AS AN ILLUSTRATION

## HOW HAS REFERENCE SERVICE BEEN TRANSFORMED IN THE DIGITAL ENVIRONMENT?

What exactly is "reference service"?

Most would say that it is helping users find the information they are looking for, or, as we have referred to it in the Introduction to this book, it is "providing access to human assistance in locating information." Others would expand the definition to include teaching users how to find the information independently. Until a few years ago, reference service was very much a face-to-face activity in which the librarian used the conversational device known as the reference interview to determine what the user really wanted to know and then selected the appropriate sources to find the answer. The face-to-face reference approach was supplemented by telephone reference, in which the reference interview was conducted without benefit of physical proximity but still allowed a one-to-one interchange between librarian and user.

Then along came the Internet, e-mail, and the Web. With the advent of remote access and distance learning, users were not only outside the building, they were not necessarily in the same state, in or near the same time zone, or even in the same country. A revolution was taking place, and *digital*—or *virtual*—reference was born.

Although libraries had for years been providing their users with selected resources or entire collections virtually, through their own Web sites, the reference transaction itself was and often still is based upon the use of e-mail or Web-based forms. In those situations, reference service may be termed *asynchronous*, that is, not carried out in real time and requiring that the user wait for a response. More and more, however, we

| Configuration | Characteristics | Pluses | Minuses |
|---|---|---|---|
| E-mail | Question can be asked any time. Response usually received within 24 to 48 hours. Often utilizes a Web form to standardize question intake process. | Does not require 24/7 staffing. Allows time to research a question. | Immediate response unlikely. Does not allow for real-time interaction between librarian and questioner. May require multiple e-mail transactions to collect the information traditionally elicited in the reference interview. Use of a Web form requires questioner to be on library Web site to submit the question. |
| "Ask a Librarian" service via a Web page | Answers can be searched for at any time using an expert system and a knowledge database containing subject-specific information or answers to previously asked questions or frequently asked questions. May be part of a comprehensive digital reference service offering e-mail and virtual live reference as well. | Fast turnaround for ready-reference type questions. Does not require 24/7 staffing. | Not real-time or interactive. |
| Real-time chat | Uses popular, readily available free instant messaging software or inexpensive shareware or open source messaging software to respond to reference questions in real time. May be operational 24/7 or have established hours when live inquiries are accepted. | Allows librarian to interact with questioner in real time. Does not require the purchase of expensive software and hardware. Simple to use. | Questioner may be inexperienced with chat software. 24/7 service requires 24/7 staffing. If shareware or open source software is used, staff will need to develop the expertise necessary to install and maintain it. |
| Virtual reference desk | Using application-specific full-featured software and hardware, either stand-alone in one institution or shared among several institutions.<br><br>More sophisticated functionality that may include audio and video conferencing, co-browsing, and Web page "pushing" in addition to live chat. More likely to be 24/7. | Interactive features create a true virtual reference desk rather than a text-based chat. | Expensive. Steep learning curve to learn software. 24/7 operation may require insourcing or outsourcing of service during overnight and early morning hours. Requires extensive planning and training, especially for collaborative projects among institutions. May require establishment of a separate physical area for virtual reference. |

**Figure 3-1. Types of Digital Reference Service**

are seeing reference service becoming *synchronous*, that is, occurring in real time, with the librarian and the user engaged in some form of interactive discourse.

Figure 3-1 lists four popular configurations for a digital reference service, along with the basic characteristics of each one and some pluses and minuses often associated with them. It also refers to "24/7" reference service—the ability to ask and answer reference questions twenty-four hours a day, seven days a week—which has surfaced as the logical outgrowth of the digital reference concept.

In essence, traditional reference service—face-to-face, building based, and generally dependent upon print—is being transformed for many libraries into a service that is also delivered virtually, on a point-of-need basis, using resources that exist in a myriad of formats that may or may not reside in the library itself. This does not mean that libraries are adopting one methodology or the other. Indeed, most libraries are creating hybrid services that incorporate elements of both traditional and digital reference services. With digital reference services, libraries often adopt a phased approach, starting with a less sophisticated, less expensive alternative—to test the waters—and then moving from there based upon user and staff feedback and experience.

What is changing for everyone, however, are the competencies required of today's reference librarian. The digital service environment has accelerated the move from task-oriented job descriptions to more competency-based descriptions, along the lines discussed in Chapter 2. The remaining sections of the current chapter will address the changing skills required of reference librarians and the move toward competency-based job descriptions.

# WHAT CHANGES FACE TODAY'S REFERENCE LIBRARIAN?

Overall, the work of the modern reference librarian has become more complex, more multifaceted than it used to be. This is not to suggest that being a reference librarian was ever a simple matter—quite the contrary. Rather, the complexity derives from the fact that at the present time, being a reference librarian means having a familiarity with software applications of varying complexity designed to facilitate re-creating the traditional, mediated instructional reference experience in an electronic environment. Furthermore, job requirements must also include the ability to interact with remote patrons in order to ascertain their needs and respond with instruction, answers, and referrals electronically.

The changes can be demonstrated by illustrating the transition from traditional job descriptions that emphasized a series of tasks to more competency-based descriptions in today's electronic environment.

- Figure 3-2 offers a brief list of generic tasks around which the traditional job description for reference work has been built.
- Figure 3-3 lists critical abilities and aptitudes associated with providing reference services in an electronic, virtual environment.

Today's reference librarian must, in fact, demonstrate skills associated with both the duties listed in Figure 3-2 and the abilities listed in Figure 3-3, hence the complexity of modern reference work—whether

---

**Duties**

- Provides reference and research assistance to library clientele.
- Interviews and interacts with clientele to establish user needs and requirements.
- Analyzes user requirements.
- Locates and selects appropriate information resources.
- Devises appropriate search strategies.
- Instructs users, either individually or in groups, on the use of various reference tools.
- Develops reading lists and subject bibliographies to meet user needs.
- Keeps abreast of appropriate review media for reference-related materials.
- Selects all types of print and nonprint media to meet the reference needs of the library's clientele.
- Evaluates the reference collection to determine materials needed.
- Obtains input from clientele to ensure that the reference collection meets their needs.
- Devises and conducts special programs that increase awareness and utilization of reference resources.
- Plans and executes timely and pertinent displays that inform clientele of the nature and scope of the library's reference collections.

**Figure 3-2. Generic Tasks Associated with Traditional Descriptions of Reference Work**

---

**Competencies***

- Possesses online communication skills and etiquette, involving chat, e-mail, and other forms of online communication.
- Is able to conduct effective reference transactions in online environments, including the creation and use of pre-scripted messages.
- Possesses Internet searching skills, in particular, the ability to choose the best starting point for online searches.
- Has the ability to search effectively as well as demonstrate the searching of library databases.
- Possesses knowledge of licensing restrictions connected with the use of library databases.
- Assists online users in applying critical thinking skills in locating, using, and evaluating information.
- Is able to conduct effectively a collaborative browsing session with a patron.
- Evaluates online reference transactions and identifies strategies for improvement.
- Is able to multitask and manage multiple windows.
- Is able to create and apply reference transaction policies in an online environment.
- Possesses technical troubleshooting skills as well as the ability to explain technical problems to facilitate diagnosis and identify solutions.
- Possesses general keyboarding abilities and is able, specifically, to make effective use of Windows keyboard commands and shortcuts.
- Has a commitment to continuous learning to improve skills in all areas of reference service.

*Source*: Derived from "Core Competencies for Virtual Reference." Olympia: Washington State Library Virtual Reference Service (n.d.). Available: http://vrstrain.spl.org/textdocs/vrscompetencies.pdf.

**Figure 3-3. Competencies Associated with Reference Work in the Virtual Environment**

---

face-to-face or virtual. In response to this growing complexity, the profession has sought to redefine what is required of a reference librarian in terms of broader competencies and specific skill sets that will allow today's practitioners to keep up with the rapidity of change and its implications for service.

# HOW DO WE MOVE TOWARD COMPETENCY-BASED JOB DESCRIPTIONS FOR TODAY'S REFERENCE LIBRARIAN?

The Reference and User Services Association (RUSA), one of the divisions of the American Library Association (ALA), has developed guidelines that deal with competencies for today's reference librarian. These guidelines reflect the professional competencies and behavioral characteristics presented in the sample job description illustrated in Source D of the Source Guide. The remainder of this chapter provides a summary of what these documents offer. (The guidelines may be read in their entirety at the RUSA Web sites that are cited in the "Sources" section of this chapter.)

The model statements of competency for reference librarians prepared by RUSA incorporate or assume a number of basic elements:

- abilities, skills, and knowledge that are unique to reference service librarians
- basic competencies required of all professionals, such as skills related to communication, reading, writing, and mathematics
- core competencies pertinent to all types of librarians
- specific behavioral performances related to approachability, interest, listening-inquiring, searching, and follow-up

**Professional competencies** are presented in terms of broadly stated goals, each of which includes a number of strategies that are action statements designed to achieve the competency goals. Figure 3-4 presents a number of the goal statements and one sample strategy for each goal.

**Behavioral performances** are presented as defining statements accompanied by specific guidelines, where appropriate, for any type of reference transaction, for in-person transactions, and for service to remote users. Figure 3-5 presents a summary of each behavioral characteristic and an example of a specific guideline for each characteristic.

Finally, it is important to remember that competencies must be developed and incorporated into job descriptions in a manner that reflects individual library needs and conditions. Societal trends and technological

| Goal statement | Example of an accompanying action strategy |
|---|---|
| A librarian provides services that are responsive to user needs. | Suggests specific works that relate to what the user said is important. |
| A librarian effectively designs and organizes reference and user services to meet the needs of the primary community. | Creates bibliographies, book talks, displays, tutorials, electronic documents, and other special tools to increase access to information resources and to motivate users to use them. |
| A librarian provides high-quality services by carefully analyzing both information sources and services. | Uses electronic and printed media to connect users with highly recommended, carefully selected sources for topics of greatest interest to primary users. |
| A librarian effectively uses new knowledge to enhance reference and user services practices. | Experiments with latest available innovations to assist users in meeting their information needs. |
| A librarian shares expertise with colleagues and mentors newer staff. | Participates in professional discussions through meetings, videoconferences, mail lists via e-mail, and other available communication methods and forums. |
| A librarian conducts research to determine what types of reference services to provide and to what types of users these services will be provided. | Conducts focus groups to meet and interact with users and to discuss and gather information about users' information needs. |
| A librarian treats the user as a collaborator and partner in the information-seeking process. | Asks user's opinion and advice while working through the information transaction. |
| A librarian develops collaborative relationships within the profession to enhance service to users. | Identifies and seeks out possible partners in order to expand services to users. |
| A librarian effectively uses tools and techniques to survey users and their information needs. | Plans and conducts regular assessments of information needs of primary user groups, using various formal and informal methods. |
| A librarian evaluates the format, access, and presentation aspects of resources as part of the overall assessment of the value of tools. | Determines if there are alternative information resources that have better user interfaces. |

**Figure 3-4. Professional Competencies for Reference Librarians: Examples from the RUSA Guidelines**

changes affect all institutions in some way. Local circumstances vary, however, and strategies relating to competencies and to their formalization in position descriptions will be developed differently from place to place. The important thing is to ensure that staff members are equipped to master an increasingly complex environment. That is the subject of Chapter 4, which follows.

| Behavioral characteristic | Example of an accompanying specific guideline |
|---|---|
| **Approachability**—librarian's initial verbal and nonverbal responses that set the tone for communication with the patron. | Librarian remains visible to patrons as much as possible; acknowledges patrons through use of greeting, eye contact, welcoming body language. |
| **Interest**—librarian must demonstrate a high degree of interest in the reference transaction. | Librarian maintains or re-establishes "word contact" with the remote patron in text-based environments by sending written or prepared prompts, etc., to convey interest in the patron's question. |
| **Listening/Inquiring**—librarian must be effective in identifying patron's information needs and in a manner that keeps patrons at ease. | Librarian uses open-ended questioning techniques to encourage patrons to expand on the request or present additional information. |
| **Searching**—working closely with the patron, the librarian must construct a competent and complete search strategy. | Librarian uses appropriate technology (e.g., co-browsing, scanning, faxing, etc.) to help guide remote patrons through library resources. |
| **Follow-up**—librarian is responsible for determining if patrons are satisfied with the results of the search and for referring patrons to other sources, including other libraries, if necessary. | Librarians make arrangements, when appropriate, with the patrons to research a question even after the reference transaction has been completed. |

**Figure 3-5. Behavioral Performances for Reference Librarians: Examples from the RUSA Guidelines**

# SOURCES

"Guidelines for Behavioral Performance of Reference and Information Service Providers." Reference and User Services Association (ALA). 2004. Available: www.ala.org/ala/rusa/rusaprotools/referenceguide/guidelinesbehavioral.htm.
"The face of Reference Services has changed significantly since the original RUSA Guidelines for Behavioral Performance were first published in 1996. Intended to be used in the training, development, and/or evaluation of library professionals and staff, the Guidelines have subsequently been favorably evaluated by the profession, and currently enjoy widespread acceptance as standards for the measurement of effective reference transactions."
"Guidelines for Implementing and Maintaining Virtual Reference Services." Reference and User Services Association (ALA). 2004. Available: www.ala.org/ala/rusa/rusaprotools/referenceguide/virtrefguidelines.htm.

"The purpose of these guidelines is to assist libraries and consortia with implementing and maintaining virtual reference services. The guidelines are meant to provide direction, without being over-prescriptive. Variance among institutions will result in differences in the adherence to these guidelines, but the committee hopes to have cast the model broadly enough to provide a framework for virtual reference which can be widely adopted and which will endure through many changes in the ways in which libraries provide virtual reference services."

Kibbee, Jo, et al. 2002. "Virtual Service, Real Data: Results of a Pilot Study." *Reference Services Review* 30, no. 1: 25–36.

The study of a pilot project at the University of Illinois at Urbana-Champaign tests the feasibility of real-time interactive reference. User feedback is positive, and valuable data is gathered to assist in future planning.

Lankes, R. David, ed., et al. 2000. *Digital Reference Service in the New Millennium: Planning, Management, and Evaluation.* New York: Neal-Schuman.

This collection of essays is the result of the "Reference in the New Millennium" Conference held at Harvard University in 1999. The papers address both the conceptual and the practical aspects involved in defining digital reference and planning, implementing, and managing a service.

Lipow, Anne Grodzins. 2003. "The Future of Reference: Point-of-Need Reference Service: No Longer an Afterthought." *Reference Services Review* 31, no. 1: 31–35.

This article "looks back" at reference librarianship from the year 2020. The author uses this technique to encourage librarians to invent their future by creating new images and directions for the work they do.

Meola, Marc, and Sam Stormont. 2002. *Starting and Operating Live Virtual Reference Services: A How-To-Do-It Manual for Librarians.* New York: Neal-Schuman.

This complete and detailed manual focuses on live virtual reference, but much of the information included in it will be relevant to other types of digital reference service. Of particular interest are the sections on planning, staffing models, and training.

"Professional Competencies for Reference and User Services Librarians." Reference and User Services Association (ALA). 2003. Available: www.ala.org/ala/rusa/rusaprotools/referenceguide/professional.htm.

"The purpose of the guideline . . . is to provide librarians, libraries, and information centers with a model statement of competencies essential for successful reference and user services librarians. Competencies must be relevant to the particular job requirements. Therefore, individuals and organizations applying these guidelines may wish to select those strategies for meeting the competency goals that are most appropriate to their situation."

Stemper, James A., and John T. Butler. 2001. "Developing a Model to Provide Digital Reference Services." *Reference Services Review* 29, no. 3: 172–89.

This article discusses the development of a model for digital reference service in a large university library system. Particular emphasis is placed on the importance of implementing digital reference in order to properly support a growing clientele of remote users taking distance education classes.

"Virtual Reference: A Work in Progress." 2004. Available: http://montanalibraries.org/textdocs/vrshistory.pdf.

This site offers a brief history of virtual reference and thoughts on its future direction. The material is part of the Washington State Library's *Anytime, Anywhere Answers: Building Skills for Virtual Reference* (http://wlo.statelib.wa.gov/services/vrs/training.cfm). A useful *Internet Reference Competencies* checklist, containing thirty-five items that can be used as a self-assessment tool, is available at http://montanalibraries.org/textdocs/internetref.pdf.

# 4 FACILITATING THE MOVE TO COMPETENCY-BASED STAFFING: CREATING A GUIDE TO PLANNING AND TRAINING

## WHAT ARE THE KEY ASSUMPTIONS IN DEVELOPING COMPETENCY-BASED STAFFING?

As we saw in Chapter 2, competencies needed by libraries for effective service are inclusive and wide-ranging. Many are related to understanding and mastering technologies; others are more broadly professional and personal in nature. Every library's needs are different, but almost all libraries in the electronic age have a growing need for competencies that will facilitate the merger of virtual services with existing print-based services in a comprehensive and cohesive service program.

This suggests that developing competencies and skills is not a simple matter. Given the complexities involved, as well as the potential costs of maintaining a multifaceted training effort, three assumptions can be made:

1. Library administration must develop and sustain its commitment, both organizationally and financially, to having library staff take the time to learn new skills and retool existing ones.

2. Training and retraining must become an inherent feature of life in our libraries, as opposed to a series of one-shot or ad hoc experiences that may be valuable in and of themselves but are not ongoing or sustained over time.

3. Libraries will have to develop a mix of training strategies, approaches, methodologies, and tools in order to have a successful program that addresses all the library's needs.

The purpose of this chapter is to present an overview of the essentials of planning a program for developing skills and expanding knowledge among staff in the modern library. We will use technology training as the focus, concentrating on planning basics that are applicable across all types of libraries. The chapter will not deal with operational and logistical details of a training program. These may be found in numerous print and Web-based sources, some of which are cited at the end of this chapter.

## WHAT IS THE ROLE OF MANAGEMENT IN MOVING TO A NEW LEARNING ENVIRONMENT?

Peter Jordan states simply that "for training to be effective, it must be viewed as an essential element in the management cycle" (Jordan 2002, 183). An excellent example of this premise is the management philosophy of the Canada School of Public Service, whose home page on the Web is cited in the Sources section of this chapter.

The school serves as Canada's "common learning service provider" for the nation's public servants. It views its mission as providing a unified approach to ensuring that all public service employees have the knowledge and skills they need to serve the country effectively. In 1999 the school created a Learning and Development Committee to "cultivate a Public Service–wide learning organization" with a mandate to ensure that, among other things, "learning becomes part of an integrated people-oriented agenda."

The Learning and Development Committee's premises are as follows:

- Knowledge and the know-how of people are the lifeblood of healthy organizations in the knowledge age.
- Human capital is to the knowledge age what physical capital was to the industrial age.
- Learning is about creating knowledge and know-how and converting it into ideas that work.
- Learning is a tool for cultural change.

From these premises, the Learning and Development Committee identified what is essentially a management commitment to learning and change:

- Develop a clear commitment of time and resources to the lifelong learning of employees.
- Ensure that all employees who wish to have a personal learning plan will have one by a specified time.

- Establish measurable targets against which to mark progress, with increases in training and development expenditures over a defined period of time.
- Identify fundamental corporate requirements and knowledge needs of managers and develop accessible learning opportunities to meet those needs.
- Encourage and support efforts of employees to improve and enhance their professional qualifications through education.
- Report annually on the progress of the learning and development effort.

Recognizing barriers to learning, such as the high cost, the difficulty in identifying and accessing appropriate learning opportunities, and scheduling conflicts, the Learning and Development Committee proposed the development of a single online learning resource covering a wide range of topics. Three components of this resource were identified:

- A learning portal with comprehensive information and a suite of online self-assessment tools to help develop individual learning plans
- A library of online learning resources, with a mix of commercially produced e-learning products and custom designed courses
- An e-learning infrastructure that manages individual learning plans, delivers courses, and keeps track of progress

The point of this example is that innovation and learning are linked and are essential to the provision of effective service. For this to occur, management must make a commitment to both the philosophy and the implementation of a program.

# HOW DO WE DECIDE ON THE ELEMENTS OF AN EFFECTIVE PROGRAM?

A major aspect of planning the move to competency-based staffing is deciding what kinds of training you need. Any given library involves a disparate set of jobs and responsibilities undertaken by a unique mix of managers, professionals, paraprofessionals, support staff and technical personnel, full-timers

| Skill | Current Level of Experience | | | |
|---|---|---|---|---|
| | None at all | Little/basic | Average | Extensive |
| Operational skills | | | | |
| Turn on the computer | | | | |
| Reboot the computer | | | | |
| Creating and saving a file | | | | |
| Copying a file from the hard drive | | | | |
| Downloading a file | | | | |
| Using a mouse | | | | |
| Selecting/working with menu items | | | | |
| Exiting Windows/shutting down | | | | |
| | | | | |
| Using software applications | | | | |
| Word processing (Word) | | | | |
| Spreadsheet (Excel) | | | | |
| E-mail/calendar (Outlook) | | | | |
| | | | | |
| Accessing and surfing the Web | | | | |
| Launch a browser | | | | |
| Use a search engine | | | | |
| Perform a search | | | | |
| | | | | |
| Performing specialized tasks | | | | |
| Complete a survey or form online | | | | |
| Bookmarking | | | | |
| Organizing "favorite" sites | | | | |
| E-mail | | | | |

(*The survey can include questions on types of training, training formats, and subject matter of additional training desired by the responder.*)

**Figure 4-1. Assessing Technology Skills: Elements of a Survey**

and part-timers. You must determine what people already know, what skill sets are in place, and what must be learned or mastered.

There are informal ways to determine these things.

- One way is observation—for example, taking note of strengths and weaknesses that manifest themselves in how work is performed in the library.
- One-on-one or small group conversations with staff members are another such method.
- Group planning meetings, at which the issue of training is brainstormed and a plan developed based upon the ideas that emerge, represent a more formal approach.

Each of these techniques has potential merit. However, the approach that is likely to yield the most in terms of generating important data for further planning is to conduct a written survey. The Southeast Florida Library Information Network (SEFLIN), seeking to develop a training program for its twenty-five-member libraries and library systems, sent a survey instrument to all staff members. The survey combined "check-off" responses with more open-ended questions designed to ascertain what skills library staffers already possessed and what things staff members felt they needed to learn. The questionnaire listed a number of tasks and skills, and respondents were asked to rate their "experience level" for each of these.

Figure 4-1, containing elements of a sample questionnaire, reflects the approach used in the SEFLIN assessment instrument. Its purpose is to illustrate one particular method for determining what kinds and levels of technology-related skills and knowledge staff members perceive themselves to have so that an effective, needs-based training effort can be established. Actual content will vary based upon the library's needs and the progress of technology at the time the survey is undertaken.

# HOW DO WE IMPLEMENT A STAFF DEVELOPMENT PROGRAM?

As the Canada School of Public Service experience suggests, libraries will likely need to adopt an array of training strategies to address different learning styles as well as budgetary and scheduling issues. Strategies may be grouped under three major types:

- Workplace training and development, including in-house training using staff already versed in the area(s) of training or hiring an outside trainer to develop a workplace-based program

- Off-site, face-to-face contracted training and development, including partnering with other libraries and sending staff to outside commercial training organizations, as well as less formal approaches such as lectures, conferences, and demonstrations

- Web-based training and development, including both instructor-led and self-study approaches that may include electronic discussions as well as the use of traditional self-paced instructional devices such as videotapes and workbooks

Whatever mix of approaches is used, the literature suggests that there are a number of important characteristics that define a successful staff development program:

- The program must have sustained support from library management and a budget sufficient to support the ongoing activity.

- The scope of instruction must adequately reflect the trainees' actual use of technology and the goals identified as a result of the assessment of staff needs.

- The program must be flexible enough to accommodate the staff members' personal needs and schedules, and it may include provisions for stipends, credits, or other incentives, as appropriate to the situation.

- The program must be carried out by colleagues or outside instructors who are proficient in teaching adults and who are conversant in effective teaching strategies for the target audience.

- Instruction should involve the trainee throughout the training experience, including the use of interactive exercises and giving trainees the opportunity to practice what they are learning.

- Instruction should be supplemented by handouts and supporting materials that allow the staff trainees to review what they have learned when they are doing their jobs.

Another important aspect of planning is to ensure that someone is available to *do* the planning! Most libraries lack the resources to hire a person whose sole responsibility it is to develop and implement a training program. Still, someone—or perhaps a team—must take responsibility for coordinating, overseeing, and evaluating the effort. Figure 4-2 lists the principal duties that characterize the coordinating of a staff-training program.

Finally, a critical element of any program is ongoing monitoring and evaluation, especially in light of the rapid changes in technology. We can identify two basic purposes in evaluating a technology-training process:

- To find out if a given strategy is effective by identifying its strengths and weaknesses
- To determine if and how the trainees' skills and their work have been affected by the training experience

The Southwest Florida Library Network (SWFLN) has identified four components in its evaluation process (see Sources for citation):

- A **"Core Competency Survey"** designed to identify skills that have been mastered and those that remain to be learned
- **"Workshop Evaluations,"** or, by extension, an evaluation of any particular training experience designed to

---

- Participate in the development of policies, procedures, and resources relating to staff development.
- Oversee the planning process and coordinate with staff managers and supervisors.
- Establish and carry out a needs assessment effort to direct the program.
- Implement a multifaceted strategy using different approaches.
- Prepare and monitor a training budget.
- Develop or participate in the development and maintenance of the training portion of the library's Web page.
- Conduct train-the-trainer workshops in support of all in-house training.
- Maintain ties with local and community organizations that offer training opportunities.
- Stay abreast of new technologies, enhancements, and developments that can affect and improve the training program.
- Monitor, evaluate, and as needed modify the program.
- Report regularly on and document the program to ensure effective communication about and support for it among library departments.

**Figure 4-2. Responsibilities and Duties in Coordinating and Implementing a Staff-Training Program**

identify the level of participant satisfaction with the training experience and their perceptions of what they learned

- **"Post-Training Surveys"** distributed at a specified time after the training experience to assess resulting changes in the participants' behavior and the impact on the organization
- **"End-of-the-Year Technology-Training Questionnaire,"** which seeks to assess the overall effectiveness of the technology-training program

In this chapter, we discussed the essentials of planning a staff development program. The chapter that follows discusses the alternatives of contracting out library work through *insourcing* and *outsourcing*. Libraries must face a key question: What works better, retooling the staff or insourcing or outsourcing the work? Chapter 8 presents ways of analyzing the specifics of your situation and making reasonable and productive decisions. We will argue that the decision-making process will likely involve a more complex solution that includes both retraining and a measure of insourcing and outsourcing because

1. up-to-date competencies and skills are the backbone of how an organization survives, and these must reside within the institution;
2. the needs of libraries are changing so fast that it is not possible to accomplish everything without outside assistance and/or support; and
3. at minimum, in-house staff will have to "manage" the decision to bring in outside staff or to outsource and ensure a successful outcome for the library.

# SOURCES

Canada School of Public Service. Network of Learning and Development Institutes. "Progress Report 2002." Ottawa: Canadian Center for Management Development (2002). Available: www.myschool-monecole.gc.ca/ldc/NLDI/learning_cover_e.html.
This site describes the school's initiatives in developing a common program of staff development and growth for Canada's public servants. The material is presented in four chapters constituting the school's Learning and Development Committee's progress report

detailing what has been learned to date, the progress of the initiatives proposed, what other organizations have accomplished, and future directions.

Johnson, Peggy. 1996. "Planning and Implementing a Cross-Training Program." *C&RL News* 57, no. 10 (November): 644–46.
This article offers insights on how a cross-training program—that is, "the process of teaching an individual new job skills in a position other than his or her usual one"—can both enhance skills and improve service.

Jordan, Peter. 2002. *Staff Management in Library and Information Work.* 4th ed. Burlington, VT: Gower.
Chapter 7 (pages 183–238) deals with staff training and development in the British environment. The author discusses responsibility for training and development, policies, resources, identifying training needs, monitoring and evaluation, stages of training, and training methods. Charts, checklists, and tables are provided.

Massis, Bruce E. 2003. *The Practical Library Manager.* New York: Haworth Information Press.
An overview of the "practical aspects of management," this book includes four chapters on building core competencies among library staff as well as planning, implementing, and evaluating technology-training programs.

Moran, Barbara, and Barbara Allan. 2003. *Developing Library Staff through Work-based Learning.* Lanham, MD: Scarecrow Press.
Revised and updated from its original publication in 1999 in the United Kingdom, this book argues that work-based learning, that is, learning-on-the-job, is "ideally suited to library and information organization settings." The volume offers tools and techniques for adopting a work-based learning program.

"SEFLIN Technology Needs Assessment Questionnaire." Fort Lauderdale: Southeast Florida Library Information Network (2002?). Available: www.seflin.org/Training/questionnaire.cfm.
This is the questionnaire referred to in the text of this chapter. It is included in Massis 2003 as well.

Southwest Florida Library Network. 2002. "LSTA Application: Technology Training."
This Library Services and Technology Act (LSTA) application for a "Technology Training" program includes useful information on the evaluation and assessment of such programs, providing the text of questionnaires referred to in the text of this chapter.

"Staff Training." Tampa, FL: Tampa Bay Library Consortium (2005). Available: http://snoopy.tblc.lib.fl.us/training/training.shtml.
This site lists training opportunities for the Tampa Bay Library Consortium (TBLC) and member library staff. The consortium's "partners in continuing education" are listed, as are links to additional

information about opportunities. The site also includes a discussion of both technology and personal competencies.

Tennant, Roy. "The Virtual Library Foundation: Staff Training and Support." Berkeley: University of California Library (1995). Available: http://escholarship.cdlib.org/rtennant/ITAL.html. "This article is the online version of the article in the March 1995 issue of *Information Technology and Libraries*." The article outlines various approaches to staff training and support, giving pros and cons of each.

# OUTSOURCING AND INSOURCING: EXPLORING THE OPTIONS AND ISSUES IN TODAY'S LIBRARY

We have referred to both outsourcing and insourcing in this book as alternatives to traditional staffing arrangements for accomplishing the work of the modern library. Libraries of all types have used both approaches extensively over the years. In fact, as the profession well knows, there is a long and sometimes controversial history of libraries contracting for goods and services with outside organizations, particularly when this has involved outsourcing specific library functions—or even the running of the whole library! We will touch on some of these issues here, but titles included in this chapter's Sources offer more in-depth material.

Definitions and assessments of these approaches vary greatly, both in the library and business literature on these subjects. This chapter offers an overview, basic definitions, and a discussion of outsourcing and insourcing as methodologies for reaching out beyond existing library staff skills for carrying out library functions.

Given the recent attention to outsourcing as a sometimes controversial element in the economic "globalization" process, this chapter will also include a section on outsourcing and its potential impact on collective bargaining and staff relations.

## HOW DO WE DEFINE OUTSOURCING AND INSOURCING?

**Outsourcing** may be defined as *using external contractors—for example, consultants, organizational partners, for-profit companies—to provide services on a long-term basis outside the library's walls.* These arrangements are typically formalized through a contract or service agreement. **Insourcing,** on the other hand, refers to the *use of outside expertise within the library to supplement internal staff resources and experience for shorter-term* *projects or over the long term.* Insourcing can involve simply bringing outside people into the organization, or it may involve having existing staff completely retrained in or refocused on other functions. A related concept is that of **co-sourcing,** whereby organizations provide a specialized service through a combination of internal resources and external expertise.

A wide array of library services have been outsourced as well as insourced over the years. Often, the outside organization is a commercial firm specializing in providing library-specific service personnel. Increasingly, not-for-profit library networks, consortia, and cooperatives have also offered services to individual libraries that may or may not be members.

Libraries began to look outside their organizations when they contracted with other libraries or service firms for the performance of traditional "back-room" technical services functions. However, the range of such services has increased as libraries entered the electronic age and as provision of new services has increasingly strained budgets. Examples include services such as these:

- Shelving and filing
- Cataloging and/or processing new acquisitions
- Performing data entry
- Classifying or reclassifying parts of or the entire library collection
- Binding and preserving existing parts of the library collection
- Selecting new books or other media for the collection
- Managing business services related to payroll and accounts management
- Organizing and producing a newsletter
- Securing the services of an information broker/searcher, often for specialized research needs
- Establishing and maintaining a library Web site or constructing a specialized database
- Digitizing specialized or unique parts of the library's print collection
- Providing graphical and publicity services
- Offering continuing professional development opportunities
- Operating the library's integrated system or other in-house technology
- Implementing a new service, such as a library cafe
- Administering a grant-funded project; and

- Managing the entire library, usually at the instigation of a governing or funding authority

As the range of functions and services that are contracted out expands, it is no longer possible to assume—as it often is—that only "non-core" services should be considered eligible for contracting out, allowing the library to concentrate on its "core" business. The above list certainly includes a number of functions that relate to a library's core purpose, no matter how one might define that concept. The point is moot, however, if we use the notion from Chapter 1—namely, that the library's core business is connecting users with the information they need.

Thus, although the core/non-core issue has always been a critical component of the debate over outsourcing, it may no longer be an important consideration. The more significant question is *why* libraries choose to contract out certain of their services, whether through outsourcing or insourcing.

# WHY DO LIBRARIES OUTSOURCE OR INSOURCE?

The reasons libraries choose to look beyond their own staff to carry out certain functions are many and varied. They may be summarized by the following list of principal and often interrelated considerations:

- The library wishes to focus on services or operations where the library has strong and developed in-house staff skills while contracting out other services.

- The library needs access to expertise not available in-house or else considered too costly to develop or acquire.

- The library needs to add new staff for specific purposes without having to establish a long-term commitment, particularly in uncertain times or if the functional need is of a temporary or passing nature.

- The library wants to turn over selected operations to outside organizations that specialize in those areas and that can more readily take advantage of the latest technologies and methodologies.

- For budgetary reasons, the library needs to shift the cost of providing services from salary lines to "non-personnel" operating lines that afford greater flexibility in how monies are allocated.

- The library wants to be relieved of all employee-related tasks such as recruitment and hiring, checking references, training, managing benefits, and evaluating performance.
- The library does not want to argue for, establish, and maintain new salaried positions that also entail significant fringe benefit costs.
- The library intends to reduce operating costs by contracting with outsiders whose charges are less than what it would cost to pay regular staff.
- The library is committed to developing skills among its own staff and determines that insourcing will enable it to bring in qualified personnel who will train in-house staff as part of the contracted services.
- The library seeks to improve operations by contracting with others to improve operational efficiency or to perform services that have become too difficult to manage or are in a state of disarray.
- The library wants to move quickly to develop a new service or to deploy a new technology that would take much longer to develop in-house.

The basis for making the decision to look beyond the library's walls is often rooted in a mix of quantitative cost-benefit and subjective political or administrative considerations. An example of the latter might be a situation where an activity has been seriously troubled over time and requires a "drastic" approach to set things right. Management might elect to outsource the activity simply to separate it permanently from the internal issues or temporarily until the internal issues can be resolved.

# WHAT ARE THE IMPLICATIONS OF OUTSOURCING FOR EXISTING STAFF IN UNION AND NON-UNIONIZED ENVIRONMENTS?

A decision to outsource library operations in whole or in part has the potential for creating serious morale problems for existing staff. They may be fearful of losing their jobs or having their duties and responsibilities radically shifted and changed. A library's management culture, including the presence of a collective bargaining environment, will have much to do with how these issues are addressed and resolved.

Library employees, professional and nonprofessional, choose to unionize for several reasons. Often these are related to economics, primarily wages and benefits; but also prominent are issues involving what employees perceive to be a negative environment underscored by an adversarial management style that locks employees out of input into decision making and lacks fairness and mutual respect. This management style, whether or not it results in unionization of employees, is antithetical to the success of an outsourcing project.

## HOW DO LABOR RELATIONS AFFECT THE OUTCOME OF A CONTRACTED SERVICE?

For outsourcing to succeed, it is very important to involve all the stakeholders in the planning and decision making, including the selection of vendors and the creation and monitoring of contracts. In a unionized library in which the collective bargaining environment has moved past adversarial, win-lose negotiations to a more collaborative, problem-solving atmosphere in which union representatives and management meet regularly to identify and discuss issues, the structure is already in place to facilitate shared planning and implementation of an outsourcing project. Under these circumstances, a union will be a powerful partner in providing employees a participatory avenue, utilizing the techniques of win-win negotiating and consensus bargaining to give all parties a voice in the process and implementation.

The presence of collective bargaining contracts at first glance might seem to be an impediment to a library's decision to outsource. It is true that the necessity to negotiate may make it more difficult to move quickly in the direction of outsourcing, but in fact speed in this context may not be in the library's best interest. The experience of the Hawaii State Library's outsourcing of collection development and associated technical services functions for Hawaii's public libraries to Baker and Taylor in 1996 has become the poster child for how not to outsource. The project was planned, approved, contracted, and implemented between August 1995 and March 1996. The librarians affected by the decision to outsource were not consulted at any point during the process. The project failed utterly and was terminated by a bill passed by the Hawaii state legislature sixteen months later.

An outsourcing project conceived, developed, and implemented in a workplace characterized by entrenched, adversarial attitudes has much less chance of success than one developed in an atmosphere emphasizing collaboration, consensus building, and win-win negotiating strategies. As a result, non-unionized libraries with top-down management styles and libraries with union-management relationships based on deep-rooted adversarial positions will need to spend considerable time and effort effecting changes in their institutional culture and in the attitudes of their staffs before moving forward with a concept for outsourcing library functions.

In contrast, non-unionized libraries with management committed to goals of collaboration, fairness, and consensus building, as well as libraries with union contracts built on consensus bargaining and yes-yes negotiations, will be well positioned to approach outsourcing from a position of strength and collaboration on the part of both management and employees. Such approaches offer better prospects for meeting the challenges involved in outsourcing and following them through to a successful implementation.

# WHAT ARE THE BENEFITS AND CHALLENGES IN OUTSOURCING OR INSOURCING?

A recurring theme with outsourcing and insourcing is the question of benefits and challenges for libraries. Much of the literature is devoted to this complex question. In a later chapter, we will look specifically at costing issues and at ways of comparing the costs of outsourcing or insourcing with the costs involved in using library staff.

Generally, benefits associated with outsourcing and insourcing include

- providing better or enhanced service,
- acquiring knowledge or expertise that is not available among the library's staff, and
- having the flexibility to move quickly or in a certain direction to provide a new service.

Challenges focus on

- struggling to integrate, administratively, the outsourced or insourced activity with other activities performed by regular staff,
- having difficulty ensuring that contracted personnel have the same commitment to performing at a high level of quality as do your own staff, and
- losing control of how and when the work is done.

In fact, as suggested by the examples offered in Figure 5-1, the upsides and downsides of contracting out library functions are often two sides of the same conceptual coin.

| Reason for outsourcing or insourcing | Potential benefit to the library | Potential challenge to the library |
|---|---|---|
| Library outsources the management of its integrated system. | Library is freed from having to hire specialized staff or worrying about day-to-day concerns. | Library loses control over key decision making as it relates to its system. |
| Library insources digitization specialists to convert print holdings. | Library does not need to hire new staff or undertake expensive training of existing staff. | Existing staff may feel threatened by insourced personnel who the staff feel may be displacing them. |
| Library contracts with local consortium to coordinate and manage a new grant-funded collaborative project. | Library moves in new service directions and strengthens ties with other libraries in a new partnership. | Pressures of starting up a new service and funding it over the long term have an impact on traditional service program. |

**Figure 5-1. Benefits and Challenges in Outsourcing and Insourcing—Three Examples**

✓ Spell out clearly what you expect to accomplish through the contracted relationship and develop written specifications accordingly.

✓ Have your specifications and contract reviewed by legal counsel.

✓ Make sure that your specifications include standards that you intend your contractor to follow.

✓ Make sure that your contract includes monitoring arrangements as well as procedures for resolving problems and disputes.

✓ Make sure that your contract has sufficient flexibility if changes are required.

✓ Make sure that reporting relationships for insourced and other contracted personnel are clearly and unambiguously spelled out.

✓ Decide ahead of time if you expect the contractor to provide any staff development as part of the work and make sure this is incorporated into the agreement.

✓ Make sure that you have communicated the purpose of the outsourcing or insourcing to your staff and that they understand (and hopefully buy into) the arrangements being made.

✓ Use your contracting out experience as a way of strengthening relationships with vendors, other libraries, and library organizations.

✓ Maintain an ongoing review of your contractual arrangements to ensure that they are compatible with the overall staffing plan for your library.

**Figure 5-2. A Contracting-Out Checklist**

One way to maximize benefits and reduce the risks inherent in outsourcing or insourcing is to develop a checklist for contracting out services that includes the important aspects of establishing a new organizational relationship. Figure 5-2 offers such a checklist.

In Chapters 6 and 7, we will attempt to put "meat on the bones" of contracting for services through outsourcing and insourcing by providing illustrations of how libraries can approach the use of these options for comparatively new service areas that may challenge the library's resources or the skills of in-house staff, namely, Web page development and digitization. In Chapter 8, we will discuss how libraries can establish a staffing plan that provides for an appropriate mix of internal and external resources. The Conclusion will offer observations on what it means to "staff" the modern library.

# SOURCES

Adelsberg, David van, and Edward A. Trolley. 1998. "Strategic Insourcing: Getting the Most from the Best." *Training & Development* 52, no. 7 (July): 57+ [4 p.].

The authors discuss the use of insourcing by companies to "overcome many of the strategic challenges and all-or-nothing limitations of traditional outsourcing." They review the use of insourcing "to blend internal and external training and development staffs," and they enumerate planning tasks necessary for strategic insourcing.

Auld, Hampton. 2002. "The Benefits and Deficiencies of Unions in Public Libraries." *Public Libraries* 41, no. 3 (May): 135–42.

This article contains essays on unions in public libraries from practitioners who have worked in unionized libraries in a variety of positions including managers, union representatives, and managers and union representatives from the same libraries. The essays are unique in that they contain perspectives from both managers and union representatives and from libraries of different sizes and in different geographical locations.

Dobb, Linda S. 1998. "Bringing It All Back Home: Insourcing What You Do Well." *The Bottom Line: Managing Library Finances* 11, no. 3: 105–10.

This article examines Bowling Green State University Library's experiences with insourcing some of its operations—detailing benefits, risks, successes, and failures involved in "adding services in a time of constant change and reemphasis."

Feld, Paulette. 2000. "Unions: Negotiating Change." *Library Mosaics* 11, no. 4 (July–August): 16–17.

The author discusses the concept of consensus bargaining and win-win negotiations and the impact of this shift in approach in management-employee relations.

Grimwood-Jones, Diana. 1996. "Contracting Out in the Public Sector—Issues and Implications." *Library Management* 17, no. 1: 11–17.

This article examines the development of contracting out library and information services in the public sector by looking at the experiences of pilot projects in the United Kingdom. The author considers some of the benefits of contracting out as well as the key issues and implications for service delivery and staffing. The article concludes with a checklist of actions relating to contracting out library services.

Hill, Cynthia. 1998. "Insourcing the Outsourced Library: The Sun Story." *Library Journal* 123, no. 4 (March 1): 46+ [3 p.].

The author looks at how Sun Microsystems converted its outsourced library into an insourced library, emphasizing problems with the outsourcing arrangement and the steps taken to insource the library with a mix of in-house and contract staff. Issues of core competencies, cost savings, and value-added services are discussed.

Hirshon, Arnold, and Barbara Winters. 1996. *Outsourcing Library Technical Services: A How-To-Do-It Manual for Librarians.* New York: Neal-Schuman.

This book is a detailed guide to outsourcing the technical services operations of acquisitions and cataloging. The book reviews evaluating current operations, the Request for Proposal (RFP) process, evaluating vendor responses, monitoring contract compliance, and dealing with the "human resource" issues involved in outsourcing.

Lesky, Cynthia. 2003. "Selective Outsourcing: A Tool for Leveraging the Value of Information Professionals." *Information Outlook* 7, no. 6 (June): 25–30.

"Outsourcing has become a standard business practice throughout American industry. Initially seen as a cost-saving tactic, it is now viewed by many companies as a long-term business strategy. . . . [The author] explains the benefits of outsourcing for information professionals."

Linder, Jane C. 2004. *Outsourcing for Radical Change: A Bold Approach to Enterprise Transformation.* New York: AMACOM.

The author compares "conventional" outsourcing to a more drastic or far-reaching "transformational" type that she defines as "using outsourcing to achieve a rapid, sustainable step-change improvement in enterprise-level performance."

Martin, Robert S., et al. "The Impact of Outsourcing and Privatization on Library Services and Management: A Study for the American Library Association." Chicago: American Library Association (2000). Available: www.ala.org/ala/oif/iftoolkits/outsourcing/outsourcing_doc.pdf.

The study team examined the outsourcing of cataloging, materials selection, and management of library operations through literature reviews and case studies of the Hawaii Public Library System and the Fort Worth Public Library System (selection) and the National Aeronautics and Space Administration and the Riverside County Library System (management).

> In general, we found no evidence that outsourcing per se has had a negative impact on library services and management. On the contrary, the evidence supports the conclusion that outsourcing has been an effective managerial tool, and when used carefully and judiciously it has resulted in enhanced library services and improved library management. Instances where problems have arisen subsequent to decisions to outsource aspects of library operations and functions appear to be attributable to inadequate planning, poor contracting processes, or ineffective management of contracts.

The study includes "an exhaustive listing of the literature for the decade of the 1990s."

McClure, James A. 2000. "Outsourcing Support Services." *The School Administrator* 57, no. 5 (May): 32–34.

The author discusses the culture changes inherent in outsourcing and the importance of involving everyone, especially employees and their union representatives, in the process.

McNew, Christina Bennett. 2005. "Outsourcing from Inside Out." *Information Outlook* 9, no. 2 (February): 23–25.

Looking at the subject on a more personal level, the author offers a "bird's eye view of different situations where contract librarians are working . . . [showing] what it is like working as a contractor and what issues contract librarians are facing."

"Outsourcing: A Public Library Checklist." Chicago: Public Library Association (August 2000). Available: www.ala.org/ala/pla/plaorg/reportstopla/outsourc.pdf.

"Over the last two decades public library managers and local officials have expressed concern about outsourcing public library functions. . . . Given the strong opposing views about outsourcing public library services, this *Checklist* offers public library managers and officials a tool for use in addressing issues related to outsourcing."

Stoffle, Carla J. "The Emergence of Education and Knowledge Management as Major Functions of the Digital Library." Cardiff, Wales: UKOLN (November 1996). Available: www.ukoln.ac.uk/services/papers/follett/stoffle/paper.html.

This lecture, delivered at the University of Wales in November

1996 discussed various aspects of knowledge management in the digital library. Stoffle addressed the organizational changes necessary for the transition to a digital library. These changes, including communication, organizational support systems, continual learning and staff development, self-managing teams and team accountability, focus on customers, driving fear out of the organization, and diversity, parallel in many respects the changes required to successfully implement an outsourcing project.

Sweetland, James. 2001. "Outsourcing Library Technical Services—What We Think We Know, and Don't Know." *The Bottom Line: Managing Library Finances* 14, no. 3: 164–76.

Through a literature review and an analysis of case studies, the author concludes that "the available research shows that arguments in favor of outsourcing are based on supposed cost and time savings, while opposition tends to emphasize quality issues. Evidence as to whether outsourcing in general in fact saves money or time tends to be spotty, while there is some data supporting concerns about a decline in quality in many outsourcing projects."

Wilson, Karen A. "Planning and Implementing an Outsourcing Program." Chicago: American Library Association (February 1997). Available: www.ala.org/Template.cfm?Section=outsourcing &Template=/ContentManagement/ContentDisplay.cfm&Content ID=42935.

"This introduction to library technical services outsourcing describes the major steps that librarians encounter in planning and implementing an outsourcing program." There are sections on evaluating existing processes and costs, designing outsourcing services, selecting vendors, negotiating contracts, evaluating vendor services, assessing outsourcing costs and savings, and "secrets for success."

Wood, Deanna D. 1999. "Librarians and Unions: Defining and Protecting Professional Values." *Education Libraries* 23, no. 1: 12–16.

This article discusses the reasons for unionizing in libraries and also points out some reasons not to unionize. Emphasis is placed on adversarial conditions in the workplace as a reason to institute collective bargaining.

# PLANNING THE USE OF CONTRACTED SERVICES: ENSURING A LIBRARY'S PRESENCE ON THE INTERNET

## HOW DO WE ENHANCE THE LIBRARY PRESENCE ON THE WORLD WIDE WEB?

Few libraries had Web sites when the graphical browser was created in 1993. In the years that followed, however, most libraries developed a presence on the World Wide Web through their own home pages. As of 2004, there were over 7,200 pages from libraries in over 125 countries (Dowling 2004).

A 1999 Association of Research Libraries study (SPEC Kit 246 in the Sources section) cites three phases of library Web site development that still holds true for most libraries:

- An **"outreach"** period (where we were):

    - Libraries publicize traditional information about their programs and services.

    - Libraries place their emphasis on posting hours of service, providing location/direction information, creating links to an online catalog, and announcing library programs.

- A more **"user-centered"** approach (where we are today, for the most part):

    - Libraries enhance their sites with a wider array of useful information and services, such as

        - establishing virtual "24/7" interactive reference services

        - offering electronic course reserves (in academic libraries)

- posting information about newly acquired materials
- mounting "exhibits" of special collections
- maintaining links to resources beyond the library's walls
- A more **"personalized"** set of services that builds on the user-centered approach (what we are evolving toward):
  - Libraries use Web tracking and measurement tools to design individual user profiles based upon past use and articulated interests.
  - Libraries customize the site with profile-driven interfaces and other resources with an individualized focus, such as career information, news alerts, or research pages.

Whatever phase of development a library's Web site may be in, there is no quarreling with the growing importance of such sites to the future of libraries. Marshall Breeding has noted that "in today's world, a library's presence on the Web ranks only slightly behind its building in shaping users' impressions" (Breeding 2004, 40). Consequently, the critical nature of library Web site development poses a major challenge to library planning.

# WHAT ARE THE MAJOR WEB SITE DEVELOPMENT PLANNING ISSUES?

Web site development requires careful deliberation and the sustained involvement of staff and stakeholders if the library is going to get the most out of its site. Indeed, since the site represents the library to the world, planning it can raise questions about the library's strategic goals, its constituency—who the library serves, how it provides services, and why it is organized the way it is. Figure 6-1 offers a list of broad, basic questions confronting library Web site planners. The list is suggestive of the many planning questions that libraries face in constructing an effective site.

The last question in Figure 6-1 brings us to the issue of staffing. Once the library determines how a Web site will serve its purposes, it must address how and by whom it will be built and maintained. A needs assessment process will help to determine if the necessary staffing skills exist in-house. Key questions include these:

**W**hat is the objective of the library Web site?

**W**ho is (are) the target audience(s)?

**W**hat messages does the library want to communicate through its site?

**W**hat services and features does the library want to offer or make available through the site?

**W**hat kind of printed material, graphics, and art work does the library want to include on the site?

**W**hat should the site look like in terms of overall layout and design?

**I**s there a budget for the site?

**D**oes the library have the technological resources, for example, adequate servers, to maintain a site?

**D**oes the library have the human resources to create and maintain a Web site?

**Figure 6-1. Major Web Site Development Planning Questions**

- Assuming that the library has the servers it needs for a Web site—a major assumption—does the library have the staff to run and maintain them?
- Will the staff need additional training for this purpose?
- Does the library have staff with the necessary Web design skills?
- Does the library have existing staff to sustain the site once it is built?

# WHO DOES THE WORK?

Many libraries are in the position of trying to figure out if they can build and maintain a Web site using in-house staff, as well as manage the delivery of services through their Web site once it is built. Librarians already in the field are developing Web-development skills. New graduates, with skills learned in library school, are in heavy demand. Some libraries are able to hire someone full time to manage the Web site. Smaller libraries assign the job to a staff member with other responsibilities. Libraries are also experimenting with ways by which the Web site developer collaborates with others on the staff to ensure the maintenance of a quality site.

Figure 6-2 offers a list of responsibilities and qualifications for a "Web-master." The title may vary, but the job responsibilities are the same. In a library where responsibilities are distributed among several people—for example, a reference or systems librarian, part-time staff, or student aides—these components of the job may likewise be carried out by different people in a collaborative environment. However, *integration of responsibility must occur at some point if the site is to be properly maintained*. The focus of this list, therefore, is the scope of such an "integrating" responsibility rather than on technical and operational details, which will vary from library to li-

---

**Primary objective:**

Determine the requirements for the library's home page on the World Wide Web and work with others as needed to carry out the development and operation of the library's Internet presence.

**Responsibilities**

- Develop and articulate the overall focus and concept for the library's home page, in accordance with library priorities and objectives.
- Develop and maintain a strategic plan for the library's Internet presence, based upon library priorities and goals.
- Act as an entrepreneur and catalyst, stimulating interest in the home page and identifying opportunities for using the Internet to facilitate library initiatives.
- Meet regularly with library staff, both as a group and individually, to develop specific plans for their participation in developing the library's Internet site.
- Coordinate the library's Internet presence with other related systems, within and outside the library, containing public information.
- Develop, research, lay out, write, and edit home page sections and features.
- Search and review new links, ensure timeliness and accuracy of existing links, and review requests from other webmasters to link to their sites.
- Meet regularly with systems staff to design the home page, address and resolve technical problems, and evaluate new directions and technology.
- Develop tutorials and training opportunities for those individuals wishing to design and author their own Web documents.

**Figure 6-2. Responsibilities and Qualifications for a Library "Webmaster"**

- Approve all Web documents for inclusion in the library home page.
- Research new Web features and tools that might be useful for authoring documents and managing the site.
- Create opportunities for demonstrating the home page to outside user groups, both for feedback and for public relations.

**Qualifications**

- Able to function in a WIN/UNIX/Macintosh environment
- Experience with installing, operating, managing, and/or contributing HTML-encoded content to World Wide Web servers, including experience with style sheets, templates, complex tables, frames, and image maps
- Working knowledge of page composition, page layout, presentation software, scripting, mark-up editors, graphics editors
- Experience with configuring and using Internet-related software on a variety of platforms
- Experience integrating Web applications with database and legacy systems
- Familiarity with library metadata standards, including MARC and XML

**Figure 6-2. Responsibilities and Qualifications for a Library "Webmaster" (*Continued*)**

brary. Furthermore, a complete job description would also include references to broader competencies that we discussed in earlier chapters.

A library may feel that it lacks the resources to develop or hire staff to maintain a Web site. Should the library outsource or insource its Web site development needs? As Figure 6-2 suggests, contracting for services can involve anything from basic programming through graphic design to actually building the library's pages.

Figure 6-3 lists key questions a library needs to ask when deciding what services should be contracted out.

Figure 6-4 elaborates on the questions listed in Figure 6-3 with a more detailed checklist of issues that must be part of an agreement for contracting out a library's Web site. The checklist is not meant to be comprehensive but serves to illustrate what is important when libraries seek to contract out the development of their Web sites to third-party developers. Actual contracts should, of course, be formulated with the advice of legal counsel.

Here is a summary of the key areas contained in Figure 6-4:

- **Ownership and intellectual property rights.** The development agreement should clearly address the issue of

- Does the library need database programming? Will library users be querying a database? Will the library want forms? If so, will the library want its users to interact with the site or only collect information?
- Will the library want an outside company to provide a Web server and all the software, hardware, and personnel that go along with it to ensure operation of your Web site, including back-up servers and public access to the library site seven days a week, twenty-four hours a day?
- Does the library want an outside company to create Web pages using existing text and documents?
- Does the library want an outside company to provide graphics, including pictures and logos?
- Does the library want an outside company to develop a search engine?
- Does the library want an outside company to maintain the site, that is, create a directory structure for the library's Web files, to maintain, upload, and revise the library's Web files on a server?

**Figure 6-3. Key Questions for Determining the Scope of Contracting Out a Library Web Site**

**A. Ownership and Intellectual Property**

1. All screens, graphics, domain names, content, and the look-and-feel of the site developed will be owned solely by the library, together with all underlying software, object code, digital programming, source code, and the like.

2. All intellectual property developed in connection with the site will be owned solely by the library.

3. The developer, in developing the site, will not infringe or violate the copyright and other intellectual property rights of third parties.

4. If the developer is bundling or using any prior intellectual property that it owns and of which it wishes to keep ownership, the library will receive a perpetual, irrevocable, worldwide, royalty-free transferable license to the same.

5. The developer is responsible for securing various rights, licenses, clearances, and other permissions related to works, graphics, or other copyrighted materials to be used or otherwise incorporated in the Web site.

6. A copyright notice will be displayed on designated parts of the library's site.

**Figure 6-4. A Checklist for Contracting Out Web Site Development**

**B. The Development Process**

1. There must be a timetable and budget for completion of the site, including specific payment milestones as progress is made on site development.

2. There must be a mechanism allowing for change orders by the library regarding the specifications for the site, without the change orders resulting in exorbitant extra costs or delays.

3. The developer must provide alternative screen page shots for the library to review and decide upon.

4. The developer assumes responsibility for transferring the site—including all software—to the library's server and (if applicable) agrees to oversee the site's installation on that server.

5. The developer must commit to a period of testing of the site and a subsequent period during which the library may evaluate the site on its premises to make sure the site functions as anticipated and in accordance with the agreement.

6. The library will have the right to reject the site if it does not meet designated specifications and have options regarding corrections at the time of a rejection.

7. The developer will timely provide documentation and source codes for all software associated with the site.

8. As requested by the library, the developer will train employees of the library to use and maintain the software associated with the site, both initially and at the time of each upgrade.

**C. Functionality of the Site**

1. The developer will use the most current standards of technology in developing the site.

2. There must be a maximum download time for any Web page.

3. The developer must include a user option for a low-graphics version of the site in order to minimize download time.

4. The desired speed and bandwidth of the Internet connection must be specified.

5. The site must be compatible with the latest versions of Internet browser software, especially the Microsoft, Netscape and AOL browsers.

6. The site will be functioning twenty-four hours a day, seven days a week, except for scheduled maintenance or downtime.

7. The number of users that will be able to simultaneously access the site as well as response time for user requests must be specified.

**Figure 6-4. A Checklist for Contracting Out Web Site Development** (*Continued*)

8. The contract must specify how the site will be properly integrated with the library's other systems, such as an integrated library systems, intranet, or other data server structure.

9. Additions, corrections, or modifications to the site may be made by the library without interference with site operations.

10. The contract must specify security safeguards, procedures, and firewalls that the site must contain.

**D. Problems and Corrective Measures**

1. The contract must outline the developer's duty to fix any bugs and failed links, including maximum time for correction.

2. Any revisions of the site must comply with functionality specifications.

3. Any particular warranties or disclaimers by the developer must be specified.

4. The developer agrees to ensure that the software for the site is free of any viruses or disabling devices.

5. The rights of the library for termination of the agreement and the liability of the developer upon such termination must be specified.

**E. Confidentiality and Other Provisions**

1. The developer will, if requested by the library, publish information about the site with a mutually agreeable set of search engines and directions.

2. The developer will not, during the site development or thereafter, use the library's trademarks, service marks, or logos, except with the library's express written approval.

3. The developer will not use its service affiliation with the library for its own promotional purposes without prior written consent.

*Source*: Adapted from Harroch, Richard. "Checklist of Issues for Web Site Development Contracts." Available: www.electroniccourthouse.com/legaldirectory/toolsforms/checklist_of_issues_for_web_site.htm.

**Figure 6-4. A Checklist for Contracting Out Web Site Development** (*Continued*)

ownership of and intellectual property issues related to the content, screens, software, and information developed for the library's site.

- **The development process.** The development agreement should address various issues associated with the development of the site, acceptance procedures, and progress payments.

- **Functionality of the end product.** The development agreement should clearly specify the anticipated functionality of and technological requirements for the site.
- **Problems that may require corrective measures.** The development agreement should address the problems with the site that may arise and the developer's duty to promptly correct such problems.
- **Confidentiality.** The development agreement may impose a variety of additional duties on the developer, including the maintenance of confidentiality regarding the site's development.

# HOW DO WE COORDINATE STAFF RESOURCES FOR WEB SITE DEVELOPMENT?

Given the importance of Web site development for libraries—the site serves as the library's advertising, its storefront, delivery system, customer support, and service program—the site's development must be subject to thoughtful planning and decision making. It is reasonable to conclude that the skills associated with site development are becoming increasingly important and that the library itself must assume responsibility for its own site. Libraries may have the resources to do it all themselves, or they may need to contract out all or part of the process. Content and control must stay with the library. This means that the library must, at minimum, assume responsibility for decision making relating to content, must have in-house knowledge of the issues involved in maintaining control, and should make the effort to train staff for doing the work on-site or managing the work accomplished through outsourcing or insourcing.

# SOURCES

Breeding, Marshall. 2004. "Essential Elements of a Library Web Site." *Computers in Libraries* 24, no. 2 (February): 40–42.
    As the title suggests, this article discusses the essential elements necessary to create an effective and useful library Web site. It is

also available on Breeding's Web site, "Library Technology Guides," http://www.librarytechnology.org/ltgdisplaytext.pl?RC= 10780.

Clark, John. 2000. "Libraries' Electronic Presence at the End of the Century: A Look Back and an Assessment." *Behavioral & Social Sciences Librarian* 19, no. 1: 61–65.

This article reviews how libraries began to use the Internet as a vehicle for communication and for the sharing of information, and how libraries use Web sites as a means for making new resources available and accessible to users.

Dowling, Thomas. "LIBWEB: Library Servers via WWW" OhioLINK (2004). Available: http://lists.webjunction.org/libweb/.

This site tallies and provides links to the world's library home pages, with a breakdown by region and state and by countries around the world. The site allows you to do a keyword search for location, library type, name, or other information.

"Innovative Internet Applications in Libraries." Wilton, CT: Wilton Library (January 2005). Available: www.wiltonlibrary.org/ innovate.html.

This site offers an extensive listing of and links to databases, forms, guides, collections, virtual services, tours, and so forth that libraries provide through their Web sites. There is something here by and for libraries of all types.

"Staffing the Library Web Site." Washington, DC: Association of Research Libraries (November 2001). Available: www.arl.org/ spec/266sum.html.

This document, ARL SPEC Kit 266, includes, among other things, a description of webmaster responsibilities at a number of research universities as well as details of how web development committees and teams operate at certain university libraries.

"Weaving a Secure Web around Education: A Guide to Technology Standards and Security." Washington, DC: National Center for Education Statistics (NCES). April 2003. Available: http://nces .ed.gov/pubs2003/secureweb/ch_4.asp.

Although focusing on classroom education, this site has material on Web site planning issues that is useful to libraries. Chapter four deals with "Internal and External Resources for Web Development."

"Web Page Development and Management." Washington, DC: Association of Research Libraries (June 1999). Available: www.arl.org/spec/246fly.html.

Included in this discussion of ARL library homepages (SPEC Kit 246) is a consideration of the phases of Web site development in ARL libraries that is also pertinent to all types of libraries.

# 7 ARRANGING OTHER CONTRACTED SERVICES: DEVELOPING A DIGITAL COLLECTION

In this chapter, we briefly overview another area of library service that has emerged from the technology revolution, namely, the developing of digitized resources and collections. We will reiterate points about contracted services that we made in Chapter 6 and offer an approach to planning the use of such services in the library.

## WHY DO LIBRARIES DIGITIZE?

Digitization converts the format of physical materials—for example, books, paintings, and manuscripts—that may be read or observed by people to formats such as CD-ROM or online that are then "readable" by computers. Digitization is accomplished through the use of scanners and digital cameras of various kinds.

Why do libraries digitize collections? Principal reasons include

- enabling a wider dissemination of unique collections and materials that would otherwise remain inaccessible;
- making possible the searching or manipulation of materials in new ways, thereby enhancing and extending their use;
- making materials accessible "anytime, anywhere" through local systems and the Web;
- establishing links to bibliographic records and other sources of information that enhances the intellectual control of library collections;
- ensuring a longer shelf life for materials by reducing the wear and tear that result from physical retrieval and handling.

A study by the federal Institute of Museum and Library Services (IMLS) in 2002 reported that only a minority of libraries is involved in projects designed to make materials in traditional formats available in digital formats. While libraries are heavily involved in technology, only a third of academic libraries and a quarter of public libraries are involved in digitization efforts. A lack of money, perceived need, and on-site expertise were the main reasons why digitization was not proceeding as quickly as one might expect.

Still, given the expanded possibilities for access to information made possible by computers and their global interconnectivity, it is not unreasonable to imagine that at least the perception of need will change in the years ahead. We should get further insight into this when the IMLS's second survey on the status of digitization projects in museums and libraries is published. This second study was announced in July 2004, with a report due in "early 2005." The findings had not been made available as of the submission of the manuscript for this book.

# WHAT ARE THE COMPONENTS OF A DIGITIZATION PROJECT?

No two projects are alike. However, reading across the source material in this area, we can identify and summarize five basic components of a digitization project. They are as follows:

1. *Selecting materials for digitization*, that is, reviewing physical source materials that are likely candidates for digitization, such as books, sound recordings, visual media, or unique historical objects.

2. *Deciding on digitization methods*, that is, determining what has to be done with the selected materials, for example, scanning images of pages to create a digital file or encoding an existing digital file to extend accessibility and use of the material.

3. *Determining the appropriate level of technical, structural, and descriptive metadata (data about data) standards*, based upon the nature and intended use of the material, the amount and kind of description that already exists, and the audience for whom the description is intended.

4. *Establishing handling and conservation practices*, particularly as they pertain to the preservation and conservation of the physical object(s) selected for digitization.

5. *Identifying and analyzing the costs of digitization*, both the initial, project-specific costs and ongoing expenses.

**W**hat are the benefits of digitization, and how will it support the institutional mission?

**H**ow will digitization add to the information value of the physical material?

**W**hat bibliographic and metadata standards will we apply to ensure preservation and access?

**D**o we have the right to digitize the material, and are there any copyright issues?

**I**f access is the goal, who is the audience that will benefit from the project, and how will they benefit?

**A**re the resources available to sustain the results of the project over time?

**Figure 7-1. Major Digitization Planning Questions**

Generally, budget elements will include a mix of the following:

a. Staff wages and benefits
b. Staff training
c. Equipment and supplies
d. Contracted services and legal fees
e. Overhead and indirect costs, such as workspace and offices
f. Maintenance, licenses, and communications charges
g. Contingency

As with anything else, the ability to do something technologically should not be the reason for undertaking a digitization project. Libraries will digitize materials as part of their organizational goals for meeting the needs of their users—the same reason that libraries develop a Web site. Sound project planning is always the key.

Figure 7-1 lists some of the broad planning questions that must be considered before embarking on a digitization project.

# WHO DOES THE WORK?

One of the major considerations in any proposed digitization effort is deciding whether to digitize in-house with existing staff, hire an outside company, or develop a hybrid solution. The decision depends on several factors, among them

- the nature of the materials being digitized,
- the level of in-house expertise and other resources to handle such materials, and
- the relative costs involved.

Here are points to consider:

- Unless you have staff expertise on-site, or else sufficient resources to commit to what could be an extended training program, you may need to obtain the services of an outside vendor for all or part of the project.
- Even with staff expertise on-site, however, certain materials may simply be unmanageable in-house. Larger, unwieldy, or physically sensitive materials may require special handling at locations that are designed and equipped to handle them.
- Handing off the work to a contractor may seem to be a problem-free solution until you realize that outsourcing means
  - navigating a contract development process, as discussed in Chapter 6,
  - constantly monitoring the project as it moves forward, and
  - negotiating solutions to problems as they arise.
- Monitoring issues notwithstanding, you must weigh having more "control" over the entire imaging process by doing the project in-house against the costs of
  - a large initial investment in equipment,
  - network downtime,
  - equipment failure, and
  - balancing the work against the demands of other projects and responsibilities.
- Finally, if contracting out is the preferred solution, libraries should still involve their staff in various ways in order to acquire a better understanding of the technologies involved. Ways to involve staff include
  - deciding what parts of the collection are to be digitized;

- overseeing and managing the project; and, if possible,
- participating in the actual scanning activity.

In order to assess in-house versus contracting-out options as they pertain to staffing decisions, consider the roles that must be filled to undertake a digitization project. Figure 7-2 offers a worksheet that allows the library,

| **Facet of Project:**_____ | | | | | | |
|---|---|---|---|---|---|---|
| **Roles** (where applicable) | **Role Definition** | **Staff Resources** | | | | |
| (*Note*: One or more roles may be combined in a single individual, especially in smaller institutions.) | | Are skills available in-house? <br><br> (yes/no) | Is training and/or retraining required? <br><br> (yes/no) | What is the cost of training and/or retraining? | Is hiring permanent or temporary staff an option? (yes/no) | If yes, what are the costs involved? |
| Project manager | Oversees the digitization project | | | | | |
| Selector/curator of source materials | Analyzes/ decides upon materials to be digitized | | | | | |
| Scanning technician/ photographer | Does the actual work of digitizing material | | | | | |
| Data entry technician | Enters data into library's database | | | | | |
| Cataloger/ metadata specialist | Enhances bibliographic records | | | | | |
| Systems administrator | Manages electronic records and systems | | | | | |
| Programmer/ database expert/interface designer | Does coding and develops user interface | | | | | |

**Figure 7-2. Digitization Tasks vis-à-vis Staff Resources**

for each facet of a digitization project, to evaluate roles and staff skills in relation to existing staff resources and what would be required, in their absence, to develop such resources. The results may be compared to the costs and related factors involved in outsourcing the project.
Facets of the project include

- administration and oversight
- selecting materials to be digitized
- digitally converting the materials
- cataloging and creation of metadata
- quality control, including post-digitization processing

A digitization project, even for the smallest library, is likely to be a hybrid of in-house and outsourcing elements. For example, as Trevor Jones (2001) points out, even if an outside vendor completes a project or new staff is hired (or leased) to work on a digital project, permanent staff should at least learn the basic theories and practices of digitization. In all cases, project planning must allow time to teach current staff new technologies. With digitization, the loss of expertise and concomitant lack of in-house knowledge and skills could compromise the long-term benefits of a successfully completed project.

# SOURCES

"Creating Digital Collections." Knoxville: University of Tennessee Library (January 26, 2001). Available: www.lib.utk.edu/plan/plan/digplan.htm.
"Every organization should carefully consider the pros and cons of outsourcing digitization projects or conducting them in-house." The site offers pros and cons for each approach.
"Digital Best Practices." Olympia: Washington State Library (2001). Available: http://digitalwa.statelib.wa.gov/newsite/best.htm.
Under "Planning a Digital Project," the site provides a guide to the "major decision points in planning a digital project." There are two resource papers of particular interest in the Project Management section: "Staffing and Training," suggesting that in smaller organizations, each staff person will have to take on many roles; and "Vendor Considerations: In-House or Out-Source," offering points to consider for both strategies.
Institute of Museum and Library Services (IMLS). "Status of Technology and Digitization in the Nation's Museums and Libraries: 2002

Report." Washington, DC: IMLS (2002). Available: www.imls.gov/
reports/techreports/2002Report.pdf.
This report presents key findings based on a comprehensive survey
done by IMLS on the use of technology and digitization activities
in museums and libraries.

Jones, Trevor. "An Introduction to Digital Projects for Libraries,
Museums and Archives." Urbana: Illinois Digitization Institute
(May 2001). Available: http://images.library.uiuc.edu/resources/
introduction.htm.
This "technical insert" originally published for the Illinois Heritage
Association provides an overview of digital project planning, with
pertinent comments about staffing and outsourcing.

"Moving Theory into Practice: Digital Imaging Tutorial." Ithaca, NY:
Cornell University Library/Research Department (2000–2002).
Available: www.library.cornell.edu/preservation/tutorial/
management/management-03.html.
Produced by the Cornell University Library Research Department,
this site includes a section entitled "Determining the Best Approach:
Outsourcing vs. In-House Programs."

Russell, Beth M. 2001. "From the Ground Up: Lessons Learned from a
Librarian's Experience with Digitizing Special Collections."
*College & Research Libraries News* 62, no. 6 (June): 603–6.
Research libraries generally have an edge in getting started on
complex technology projects. However, the requisite skills may
have to be developed even in that kind of an environment. As such,
this article provides an encouragement to getting started and offers
a broad review of the phases involved in a digitization project.

Sitts, Maxine K. "Handbook for Digital Projects: A Management Tool for
Preservation and Access." Andover, MA: Northeast Document
Conservation Center (December 2000). Available: www.nedcc.org/
digital/dman.pdf.
This is part of the Northeast Document Conservation Center site.
Chapter III, "Considerations for Project Management," offers managers material on forming "effective strategies to design, fund, and
manage digitization projects." The chapter includes a section on deciding who will do the work and on staff roles for carrying out digitization tasks.

# DESIGNING THE MIX: CHOOSING WHAT WORKS BEST FOR THE LIBRARY

---

## HOW DO LIBRARIES TYPICALLY CHOOSE AMONG VARIOUS STAFFING OPTIONS?

The title of this chapter implies something that most libraries do not actually do—that is, develop a comprehensive staffing plan involving the various approaches that we have discussed and illustrated so far. Yet, trying to decide among these different approaches in any given situation, namely, using and retraining existing staff, outsourcing, insourcing, hiring new staff, is a realistic and practical possibility.

The question is often posed in the context of deciding whether or not to outsource. Typically, the basis of the decision is relative cost: How much can we save by farming out this job? With this in mind, Figure 8-1 (Matthews 2002) offers a table that can assist decision-makers to identify and compare costs associated with providing a service using in-house resources versus contracting it out.

By using this table, preliminary cost comparisons can be spelled out and the relative benefits, at least as they relate specifically to cost, can be understood.

The cost factors presented here may be supplemented by others or broken down further, depending upon the function involved. For example, if the analysis is for a technology support function, distinctions will have to be made between the cost of server hardware and the cost of peripheral equipment, and between application software and operating system software. For all functions, staff costs will have to include those associated with managing the function directly vis-à-vis overseeing the outsourcing or insourcing contract. Finally, the worksheet includes space for calculating more than one outsourcing or insourcing option.

| Cost factor | Existing or projected in-house costs | | Outsourcing/ insourcing Option 1—Costs | | Outsourcing/ insourcing Option 2—Costs | | Outsourcing/ insourcing Option 3—Costs | |
|---|---|---|---|---|---|---|---|---|
| | Initial | Recurring | Initial | Recurring | Initial | Recurring | Initial | Recurring |
| Professional staff Salaries | | | | | | | | |
| Professional staff Benefits | | | | | | | | |
| Support staff Salaries | | | | | | | | |
| Support staff Benefits | | | | | | | | |
| Equipment | | | | | | | | |
| Software | | | | | | | | |
| Databases | | | | | | | | |
| Telecommu- nications | | | | | | | | |
| Miscellaneous supplies | | | | | | | | |
| Training | | | | | | | | |
| Planning/ consultation | | | | | | | | |
| Other _____ | | | | | | | | |
| Other _____ | | | | | | | | |
| *Totals:* | | | | | | | | |

**Figure 8-1. A Worksheet for Comparing the Costs of Using In-House Staff and Contracted Services**

# WHICH FACTORS—BEYOND COST— ARE CRUCIAL?

Whereas these fairly straightforward considerations may work for limited functions such as copy cataloging or for sustaining an automated circulation system, the issue becomes more intricate when libraries start looking at professional-level services such as providing reference, operating multi-faceted electronic systems, or building and maintaining a Web site. Cost is crucial, but so are other factors, such as organizational culture and the impact on internal operations.

Here are two brief illustrations.

## A. Virtual Reference

In Chapter 3, we discussed the changing nature of reference service, focusing on the need for new staff competencies in an electronic or virtual service environment that includes interactions by means of e-mail and chat. As libraries transition to new ways of doing business, their staff may still be developing the requisite skill sets. In the interim, or even as a longer-term solution, libraries may turn to a commercial reference contractor, usually off-site, to handle the additional work. In addition to cost considerations, it may be necessary to weigh other issues, such as these:

- Will the staff perceive contracted services as integral to the service—or as an unwanted intrusion that conflicts with organizational values?
- Can contracted services be integrated into existing operations or must they be set up as a separate function—and how would that be perceived within the organization?
- How are the new services affecting staff-user relationships?
- Is adopting the "latest thing" in reference diverting critical resources from other library service functions?

## B. Maintaining a Local Electronic System

In the 1980s and early 1990s, local systems in libraries were automated versions of traditional library operations, particularly for circulation control functions. In the mid-1990s, the impact of the World Wide Web resulted in more complex systems that provided access to an increasing array of electronic information resources. By the early years of the twenty-first century, local systems had moved beyond bibliographic information to an array of resources and service functions with dimensions heretofore unknown in libraries—such as embedding electronic library resources in Web-based course software.

Maintaining local electronic systems moved from a part-time job added to a staff member's existing responsibilities to a full-time commitment on the part of someone formally trained in information technology skills. Some libraries hired systems librarians to manage the library's network, deal with vendor technical support, supervise other technical staff, and plan for the future. Other libraries, however, borrowed a solution from the corporate sector and contracted out system management to an *Application Service Provider*—ASP—who manages the system remotely using the Internet.

However, as with contracted reference services, there are potential questions:

- Does the parent organization support the concept of management through ASP?
- Has the library built safeguards into the ASP contract to ensure that it maintains control of its own system?
- Do the contractual services mesh effectively with technology functions that are retained and managed in-house?
- How does the use of ASPs impact on the development of skill sets by library staff?
- How is library technology planning affected by the involvement of an off-site technology "partner"?

It might also be appropriate to review the issues of staff morale discussed in Chapter 5. Any decision that affects or is perceived to affect existing staff must be considered carefully in the context of ensuring that any contracted service meshes properly with ongoing practices. If the intention is, in fact, to "upset the applecart," such a move must still be carefully planned and thought through.

## WHAT WAYS CAN WE THINK STRATEGICALLY ABOUT STAFFING OPTIONS?

In light of such questions, "designing the mix" really means thinking strategically about the staffing options available to the library. In his book on strategic planning, John M. Bryson (1995) proposes a list of considerations that planners must use "to link the organization with its environment" as they develop strategies (pp. 146–53). What this means is that thinking strategically involves considering internal, organizational and environmental factors when weighing the staffing approaches to use.

Is there a way of capturing this concept in a practical, straight forward planning process? Figure 8-2 offers a strategy-based, decision-making matrix that allows for collecting ideas and data about staffing options. The matrix expands the cost-focused analysis in Figure 8-1 and is based upon materials cited in the Sources that offer decision matrices for deciding whether to outsource. However, the range of options in Figure 8-2 is greater and uses elements adapted from Bryson's study to give decision-makers a tool with which to gather information and evaluate alternative possibilities strategically.

Figure 8-3 provides a second, accompanying matrix that takes the decision-making elements from Figure 8-2 and allows libraries to rank them in importance. This can be as basic as assigning relative point values to these elements, say 1 to 5, reflecting lesser-to-greater importance in determining how they will assist in deciding which staffing alternative(s) to choose.

These tables do not offer a magic formula that can be applied to this process. Rather, they provide a framework for thinking about options and, through brainstorming and a careful consideration of the issues, arrive at a way of deciding how best to "staff" a traditional function or a new, prospective service. It is always a subjective process, with more-or-less objective elements that help to guide the library's thinking and help to make decisions that will work for the library.

| Decision-making elements/ considerations | Use existing staff | Retrain existing staff | Outsource | Insource | Hire new staff (with new competencies) |
|---|---|---|---|---|---|
| What are the principal features of this approach? | | | | | |
| What are the intended outcomes? | | | | | |
| What is the timetable for implementation? | | | | | |
| Who is responsible for implementation? | | | | | |
| What resources are required? [list] | | | | | |
| What are the anticipated costs—initial and recurring? | | | | | |
| What savings are expected? | | | | | |
| Is the approach consistent with organizational values, culture, philosophy, or rules? | | | | | |
| Will the approach win acceptance within the organization? | | | | | |
| What will be the impact on services? | | | | | |
| What will be the impact on users or clients? | | | | | |
| How does this strategy coordinate with other strategies, programs, or activities? | | | | | |
| *Other* | | | | | |
| *Other* | | | | | |

**Figure 8-2. A Worksheet for Considering Staffing Alternatives Strategically**

| Decision-making elements/considerations | Rank/priority |
|---|---|
| What are the principal features of this approach? | |
| What are the intended outcomes? | |
| What is the timetable for implementation? | |
| Who is responsible for implementation? | |
| What resources are required? [list] | |
| What are the anticipated costs—initial and recurring? | |
| What savings are expected? | |
| Is the approach consistent with organizational values, culture, philosophy, or rules? | |
| Will the approach win acceptance within the organization? | |
| What will be the impact on services? | |
| What will be the impact on users or clients? | |
| How does this strategy coordinate with other strategies, programs, or activities? | |
| *Other* | |
| *Other* | |

**Figure 8-3. Ranking of Decision-Making Elements from Figure 8-2**

# SOURCES

Ball, David. 2003. "A Weighted Decision Matrix for Outsourcing Library Services." *The Bottom Line: Managing Library Finances* 16, no. 1: 25–30.

This article is based on a study undertaken in the UK in 2000–2001 "to give an up-to-date view of the current experience of outsourcing and externalization in libraries, museums, and archives." The author provides a weighted decision matrix for "judging the suitability of library services for outsourcing."

Barreau, Deborah. 2001. "The Hidden Costs of Implementing and Maintaining Information Systems." *The Bottom Line: Managing Library Finances* 14, no. 4: 207–13.

This article discusses some of the costs associated with implementing information systems that often do not appear on budget projections but nonetheless affect staffing and management. These include

impact on other work, training, and salary and overhead of staff involved in planning a system.

Breeding, Marshall. 2004. "Automated System Marketplace 2004:
Migration Down Innovation Up." *Library Journal* 129, no. 6:
46–58.
Breeding's annual assessment of the state of the library system
marketplace notes interesting trends regarding the use of ASPs by
libraries.

Bryson, John M. 1995. *Strategic Planning for Public and Nonprofit
Organizations: A Guide to Strengthening and Sustaining Organizational Achievement.* Rev. ed. San Francisco: Jossey-Bass.
This book offers one of the best and concise overviews available of
the strategic planning process. Chapter 7 focuses on "Formulating
and Adopting Strategies and Plans to Manage the Issues." As an extension of the organization's mission, any strategy "forms a bridge
between the organization and its environment" and must be formulated so that it can be adopted in a "politically acceptable, techni-
cally workable, and legally and morally defensible form."

Coffman, Steve, and Linda Arret. 2004. "To Chat or Not to Chat—Taking
Yet Another Look at Virtual Reference, Part 2." *Searcher* 12, no. 8
(September): 49–56. Available: www.infotoday.com/searcher/
sep04/arret_coffman.shtml.
This article looks at the costs of providing chat reference service
in libraries, concentrating on budgetary issues, but considering
non-"bottom-line" issues as well. Part 1 appeared in the July/
August issue and offers a history of chat and virtual reference in
libraries.

Lankes, R. David, ed., et al. 2000. *Digital Reference Service in the New
Millennium: Planning, Management and Evaluation.* New York:
Neal-Schuman.
This collection of essays is the result of the "Reference in the New
Millennium" conference held at Harvard University in 1999. The
papers address both the conceptual and practical aspects involved
in defining digital reference and planning, implementing, and man-
aging a service.

Marcum, James W. 1998. "Outsourcing in Libraries: Tactic, Strategy, or
'Meta-Strategy'?" *Library Administration and Management* 12,
no. 1 (Winter): 15–25.
"This article will provide background and context for the issue of outsourcing, illustrate the practice as it exists in libraries, offer a model
for analyzing outsourcing alternatives and a scenario for testing the
model, and suggest alternate approaches for managers that reach beyond the prevailing 'competitive strategy' discussion of the problem."

Matthews, Joseph R. 2002. *Internet Outsourcing Using an Application
Service Provider: A How-To-Do-It Manual for Librarians.* New
York: Neal-Schuman.

Figure 8-1 is an adaptation of one used by Matthews in this manual in which detailed material calculating the benefit components of contracting out automated services is presented.

Meola, Marc, and Sam Stormont. 2002. *Starting and Operating Live Virtual Reference Services: A How-To-Do-It Manual for Librarians.* New York: Neal-Schuman.

This complete and detailed manual focuses on live virtual reference, but much of the information included in it will be relevant to other types of digital reference service. Of particular interest are the sections on planning, staffing models, and training.

Reenstjerna, Fred R. 2001. "Application Service Providers: Can They Solve Libraries' Problems?" *Computers in Libraries* 21, no. 3: 34–38.

The author provides a brief overview of how ASPs might be used in libraries as well as a checklist of requirements for implementing a successful ASP solution.

# CONCLUSION: BROADENING THE DEFINITION OF "STAFF" IN A VIRTUAL WORLD

## WHAT HAS THIS BOOK COVERED?

In their book *Quality Management for Information and Library Managers* (London: Aslib, 1996), Peter Brophy and Kate Coulling talk about "disintermediation," that is, the removal of staff as an intermediary between library services—reference, for example—and users:

> Information technology . . . enables services to move from customer-employee relationships to customer-service direct interaction. It is helpful when analyzing these customer-service interactions to think of the customer as being (in part) an (unpaid) employee. People deliver services to themselves. (Quoted in Brophy 2001, 92)

"Users-as-staff" is a unique and challenging notion—another reflection of how technology has altered the way that libraries do business today. In the present book, we do not explore the idea that library users may assume the attributes of staff. However, we do suggest that what staff needs to know—indeed, who your "staff" are—has substantively changed in the "anywhere, anytime" library of today. The book's focus has been on reviewing

- how competencies, skills, and job descriptions have changed in response to new technologies; and
- how library functions, old and new, are increasingly performed by a mix of human resources, including—but not limited to—in-house personnel on the library's payroll.

In rethinking the traditional library environment and how work gets done in the modern library, we have sought to

- establish a framework for viewing the modern library as a "lean" organization that makes use of alternative approaches, such as outsourcing, to complement the work performed by in-house library staff;

- define and offer examples of job competencies and skills that are requisite for library staff working in the technology affected libraries of the twenty-first century;

- offer material on and examples of competency-based job descriptions that reflect the demands of providing services in an electronic, often virtual environment, with an illustrative chapter on reference services;

- describe planning issues associated with establishing a staff development program through which libraries can respond to and anticipate the need for new competencies and skills related to technology;

- discuss issues involved in contracting out the performance of library functions, illustrating the coordination and use of such services in the context of library Web page development and the digitizing of library materials;

- offer methodologies for "designing the mix" of in-house staffing and contracted services that will meet the needs of the modern library.

# HOW DO WE BEST ORGANIZE HUMAN RESOURCES FOR EFFECTIVE RESULTS?

The chapters of this book suggest that future library staffing will represent a hybrid of approaches—a "fusion" of solutions that reflects those mentioned in Chapter 1, including, for example, partnerships, alliances, and outsourcing, in addition to the use of in-house staff. We have not provided a detailed look at each of these options in the present volume, but it may be worthwhile to offer an example of how several of these elements may be brought together to expand and improve services in today's library.

QandANJ is an excellent example of how users can profit from a library service—in this case 24/7 reference service—in a more cost-effective manner through the combination of in-house staffing, collaborative, and outsourced approaches. It also serves as an example of the importance of staff training and development, since the program's success rests on the ability of reference librarians to operate effectively in a virtual environment.

> "QandANJ" (www.qandanj.org/about.htm) is a virtual reference service in New Jersey. The service employs elements of both collaboration and outsourcing to achieve its goal of offering free, live, online reference service twenty-four hours a day, seven days a week. The service is directed toward New Jersey libraries and residents of the state.
> QandANJ uses live virtual reference software marketed commercially by Library Systems and Services, L.L.C. (LSSI), and is hosted on LSSI's servers. A prime example of outsourcing, the service is based on librarians from LSSI's Web Reference Center covering overnight and weekend hours. (See www.LSSI.com and www.tutor.com.)
> However, QandANJ also incorporates elements of a collaborative model by developing a network of participating libraries of all types throughout the state through New Jersey's state-funded network of regional library cooperatives. One of these cooperatives—the South Jersey Regional Library Cooperative—serves as the administrator of the program. Participating libraries agree to staff the virtual reference desk for an assigned period of time between 9 AM and 9 PM, Monday through Thursday, 9 AM and 5 PM on Friday, and daytime hours on Saturday. During these times, between two and four librarians are on virtual duty. Each participating library covers five to ten hours per week.

Such consortial and partnering arrangements are not new, and there are innumerable variations on the theme. For example, in Chapter 8, we made mention of using an ASP as an alternative to in-house managing of an integrated system. More common, certainly, are the models of libraries joining a consortium—or smaller consortia joining larger ones—for this purpose in order to take advantage of shared costs, collaborative system management, and the shared use of technical staff. In this fashion, individual libraries and smaller organizations can avoid hiring new staff or training existing staff to cope with managing their electronic systems and services.

In short, successfully providing service in the modern library depends upon the planned and effective use of different approaches to staffing. One observer, Sabyasachi Bardoloi (2003), has used the expression "smartsourcing" to describe a mix of outsourcing and insourcing solutions to supplement in-house network support resources. Broadening the concept to include, potentially, the full array of services offered by libraries, we see in-house personnel as but one component, albeit a crucial one, of a library's staffing pattern. This is the mark of a "lean" organization in rapidly changing times.

Finally, we hope that future studies will offer in-depth case studies of how libraries decided upon and then employed a mix of staffing approaches in critical areas of library work. On the basis of such studies, more comprehensive planning methodologies can be developed incorporating more elaborate matrices for decision making—to cover stages of a project or the redesign of entire functional areas in the physical—and virtual—library of the future. Quoting James Marcum in his 1998 article:

> Can libraries be transformed? I suggest not through outsourcing. Only when we broaden the concept to encompass insourcing, partnering, networking, and continual learning

does the transformation process become central to the creation of the "cybernetic" networked libraries required to meet the challenges of tomorrow. (23)

# SOURCES

Bardoloi, Sabvasachi. "Outsourcing + Insourcing: Key to Smartsourcing?" White paper prepared by the Information Research Center, Pinnacle Systems, Inc. (April 2003). Available: www.dmreview.com/ whitepaper/WID515.pdf.

"This white paper gives an overview of outsourcing and insourcing, defining the[m] both and tries to map out the advantages as well as the challenges faced by them. . . . This paper . . . tries to analyze whether a perfect combination of both outsourcing and insourcing will lead to . . . smartsourcing!"

Brophy, Peter. 2001. *The Library in the Twenty-first Century: New Services for the Information Age*. London: Library Association Publishing.

(See Chapter 1 Sources for annotation.)

Marcum, James W. 1998. "Outsourcing in Libraries: Tactic, Strategy, or 'Meta-Strategy'?" *Library Administration and Management* 12, no. 1 (Winter): 15–25.

(See Chapter 8 Sources for annotation.)

"Virtual Reference Realities: Current Research and Customer Feedback" (2004). Available: www.sjrlc.org/PLA/PLA_2004_Qand ANJ_ web.ppt.

Created by Karen Hyman and Peter Bromberg under the auspices of the South Jersey Regional Library Cooperative, this PowerPoint presentation at the Public Library Association Conference, February 26, 2004, offers a statistical portrait of QandANJ and provides data on user interaction and satisfaction with the service.

# SOURCE GUIDE TO STAFFING THE MODERN LIBRARY

# SOURCE A: CORE AND TECHNICAL COMPETENCIES FOR LIBRARIANS (NJLA)

The competencies in Source A are from the New Jersey Library Association's "Core Competencies for Librarians" (covering professional and personal competencies) and "Technical Competencies for Librarians." The quotation here explains the relationship between the two documents. In this appendix, each competency is followed, for illustrative purposes, by one example or a combination of specific examples of the competency provided in the original document.

For the complete text of each, see the source cited.

*From*: Core Competencies for Librarians

> This document attempts to define the direction in which the profession is evolving; this direction demands greater self-awareness, self-motivation, and self-improvement and participation in the process. Individual librarians must take the responsibility for furthering the evolution of their profession, in their libraries, in their communities and beyond. . . . Expertise with and willingness to use technology is underlying all areas in the field of librarianship now. Consequently, technological skills appear as a separate checklist.

## PROFESSIONAL COMPETENCIES

- **Customer service,** e.g., understands customer needs and preferences for information which build and drive the selection of resources and services;
- **Assessment,** e.g., continually analyzes and investigates the information and service needs of the targeted customer base;
- **Knowledge of information sources,** e.g., can identify materials appropriate to customers' requirements and their abilities;
- **Resource management,** e.g., organizes materials and

resources using appropriate systems of access that are compatible with customers' needs and styles of learning;

- **Technical skills,** e.g., understands and uses the latest relevant technology to manage and deliver services;
- **Advocacy,** e.g., communicates the value of library and information services to decision makers;
- **Collaboration,** e.g., collaborates to achieve common (organizational) goals in a spirit of collegiality and mutual respect;
- **Administration,** e.g., creates a culture which promotes change;

## PERSONAL COMPETENCIES

- **Education,** e.g., continuing education is essential to update skills, keep current, broaden knowledge and integrate new techniques and methodology into everyday practice;
- **Service commitment,** e.g., is interested in the goals of customers, coworkers and suppliers and strives to provide effective support in helping them achieve these goals;
- **Flexibility,** e.g., takes risks, experiments and makes mistakes and supports this behavior in others;
- **Leadership,** e.g., sees the long view, articulates the direction clearly and enlists others to jointly work to achieve it;
- **Ethics,** e.g., protects and values patron confidentiality and organizational security;
- **Communication,** e.g., effectively shares what is learned with others;
- **Self-motivation,** e.g., takes responsibility for managing the development of one's own career . . . including a commitment to lifelong learning and periodic retooling of personal skills set.

## TECHNICAL COMPETENCIES FOR LIBRARIANS

- **Online catalog,** e.g., uses advanced searching options . . . ; understands subject heading structure . . . ; understands how search operators function;
- **Electronic resources and databases,** e.g., has familiarity with full-text periodical index(es) and how to access from within (and outside) library;

- **Internet,** e.g., knows Internet terminology . . . ; is . . . able to maneuver through library's home page efficiently . . . ; is able to participate in Web site development;
- **Instruction,** e.g., is able to conduct structured Internet and other computer classes for both the public and the staff;
- **E-mail,** e.g., utilizes e-mail efficiently and professionally to increase work-related communication;
- **Applications software,** e.g., understands and efficiently manages desktop software;
- **Computer troubleshooting/preventive maintenance,** e.g., can isolate and identify problems with hardware, checking components methodically and effectively and can communicate findings to repair person;
- **Awareness of evolving technology,** e.g., expands professional reading to include technology trends, both within and outside the field of librarianship.

*Source*: Hermann, Janie L. Hassard. "Setting the Standard: The Development of Competencies for New Jersey Librarians." Trenton: New Jersey Library Association (2002). Available: www.access.gpo.gov/su_docs/fdlp/pubs/proceedings/02pro_hermann.pdf.

# SOURCE B: COMPETENCIES FOR LIBRARIANS SERVING CHILDREN (ALSC)

The competencies in Source B are from the Association for Library Service to Children (ALSC/ALA) document entitled "Competencies for Librarians Serving Children in Public Libraries, Revised Edition." Like those in Source A, each competency is followed, for illustrative purposes, by one example or a combination of specific examples of the competency provided in the original document.

The complete text is available in the source cited.

*From*: Competencies for Librarians Serving Children in Public Libraries, Revised Edition

> Effective library service for children entails a broad range of experience and professional skills. The librarian serving children is first of all fully knowledgeable in the theories, practices and emerging trends of librarianship but must also have specialized knowledge of the particular needs of child library users.
>
> The following *Competencies* make it clear that the children's librarian must do more than simply provide age-appropriate service. Children's librarians must also be advocates for their clientele both within the library and in the larger society, and they must also demonstrate the full range of professional and managerial skills demanded of any other librarians.

## ALSC COMPETENCIES

I. **Knowledge of client group,** e.g., understands theories of infant, child, and adolescent learning and development and their implications for library service;

II. **Administrative and management skills,** e.g., participates in all aspects of the library's planning process to represent and support children's services;

III. **Communication skills,** e.g., defines and communicates the needs of children so that administrators, other library staff, and members of the larger community understand the basis for children's services;

IV. **Materials and collection development**

   A. **Knowledge of materials,** e.g., demonstrates a knowledge and appreciation of children's literature . . . ; is aware of adult reference materials and other library resources which may serve the needs of children and their caregivers;

   B. **Ability to select appropriate materials and develop a children's collection,** e.g., evaluates and recommends collection development, selection and weeding policies for children's materials . . . ;

   C. **Ability to provide customers with appropriate materials and information,** e.g., matches children and their families with materials appropriate to their interest and abilities;

V. **Programming skills,** e.g., designs, promotes, executes, and evaluates programs for children of all ages, based on their developmental needs and interests and the goals of the library;

VI. **Advocacy, public relations, and networking skills,** e.g., promotes an awareness of and support for meeting children's library and information needs through all media; develops cooperative programs between the public library, schools, and other community agencies;

VII. **Professionalism and professional development,** e.g., keeps abreast of current trends and emerging technologies, issues, and research in librarianship, child development, education, and allied fields.

*Source*: *Competencies for Librarians Serving Children in Public Libraries, Revised Edition.* Chicago: American Library Association. Association for Library Service to Children (1999). Available: www.ala.org/ala/alsc/alscresources/forlibrarians/ professionaldev/competencies.htm.

# SOURCE C: MUSIC LIBRARIAN COMPETENCIES (MLA)

By way of further comparison, we offer another set of proposed competencies, this time for the subject specialist—a music librarian. These competencies were developed in 2002 by David Hunter on behalf of the Music Library Association.

The author places these competencies in the context of adding value to the services librarians provide to users, making possible "the profession's long-term strategic advantages." Hunter acknowledges that these competencies are guidelines, not legally enforceable professional standards. However, they are critical because, as he puts it, "core competencies not only define the present, they also ensure a future for the profession."

Each competency is followed by one example or a combination of specific examples of the competency provided in the Hunter article. See the citation below for the complete article.

## MUSIC LIBRARIAN CORE COMPETENCIES

- **Professional ethos,** e.g., recognizes the diversity of musics, library users (the client group), staff and the wider community, and encourages all in their musical endeavors and enquiries;
- **Training and education,** e.g., must have course work at the higher education level in music; must have the ability to read music;
- **Reference and research,** e.g., must be highly knowledgeable concerning the content of information resources in any format;
- **Collection development,** e.g., must participate in digitization projects to ensure the long-term preservation and wider dissemination of material;
- **Collection organization,** e.g., must work to improve library data systems, with a goal of integrating circulation, acquisition, and catalog information;
- **Library management,** e.g., must control the budget for

all aspects of their libraries, including staff, acquisitions, maintenance, and information and audio technology;

- **Information and audio technology and systems,** e.g., must be familiar with developments in hardware, software, and networking, and the integration of systems and media;

- **Teaching,** e.g., must educate users (actual, virtual and potential), administrators, and donors through all appropriate means, including paper, e-mail, Web sites, classes, demonstrations, presentations, individual consultation, radio, television, recordings, performances, exhibits.

*Source*: Hunter, David. "Core Competencies and Music Librarians." Middleton, WI: Music Library Association Library School Liaison Subcommittee (April 2002). Available: www.musiclibraryassoc.org/pdf/Core_Competencies.pdf.

# SOURCE D: SAMPLE BEHAVIORAL AND COMPETENCY-BASED JOB DESCRIPTION

*The resource listed below is intended as a sample and may be adapted to meet style and use needs.*

---

## JOB DESCRIPTION

**DEPARTMENT:** Administration/Support

**JOB TITLE:** Vice President, Chief Financial Officer

**JOB CODE:** xxxx

**REPORTS TO:** President/CEO

**JOB PURPOSE:** The CFO is responsible for directing the fiscal functions of the department in accordance with generally accepted accounting principles (GAAP) and cost reimbursement principles relating to the health care industry and in keeping with the goals and objectives of the organization.

### DEPARTMENTAL EXPECTATION OF EMPLOYEE

- Adheres to Duke's Policy and Procedures
- Acts as a role model within and outside Duke
- Performs duties as workload necessitates
- Maintains a positive and respectful attitude
- Communicates regularly with supervisor about Department issues
- Demonstrates flexible and efficient time management and ability to prioritize workload
- Consistently reports to work on time prepared to perform duties of position
- Meets Department productivity standards

## ESSENTIAL DUTIES AND RESPONSIBILITIES

- Plan, develop, organize, implement, direct and evaluate the organization's fiscal function.
- Participate in the development of the organization's plans and programs.
- Evaluate and advise on the impact of long range planning, introduction of new programs/strategies and regulatory interaction.
- Develop and advise on cost and reimbursement strategies.
- Develop credibility for the finance group by providing timely and accurate analysis of budgets and financial reports that will assist the President, Board and other senior managers in managing their responsibilities.
- Enhance and/or develop, implement and enforce policies and procedures of the organization by way of systems that will improve the overall operation and effectiveness of the agency.
- Establish credibility throughout the organization and with the Board as an effective problem solver; be viewed as approachable and as a mentor to people in financial issues.
- Continual improvement of the budgeting process through education of department managers on financial issues impacting their budgets.
- Provide strategic financial input and leadership on decision-making issues affecting the organization; i.e., evaluation of potential alliances acquisitions and/or mergers and pension funds and investments.
- Optimize the handling of deposit relationships and initiate appropriate strategies to enhance cash position.
- Develop a reliable cash flow projection process and reporting mechanism.
- Participate in the negotiation of contracts.
- Continual improvement of the timeliness and accuracy of the department's cash flow and management of the billing process (A/R).
- Evaluation of the finance division structure and team plan for continual improvement of the efficiency and effectiveness of the group as well as providing individuals with professional and personal growth with emphasis on opportunities (where possible) of individuals.

- Competence in billing, general ledger software, Lotus/Access/Excel type spreadsheets and overall general knowledge of system databases and master files.
- May be asked to be responsible for management of the Department in the absence of the Vice President.

## ADDITIONAL DUTIES AND RESPONSIBILITIES

- Accomplishes all tasks as appropriate.

## QUALIFICATIONS

- **Experience, Education and Licensure.** An experienced leader and financial executive with health care experience preferably in the home health field. An energetic, "straight shooter" with high ethical standards and an appropriate professional image. A strategic visionary with sound technical skills, analytical ability, good judgment and strong operational focus. A well-organized and self-directed individual who is "politically savvy," "street smart" and a team player. An intelligent and articulate individual who can relate to people at all levels of an organization and possesses excellent communication skills. A good educator who is trustworthy and willing to share information and serve as a mentor. An excellent negotiator who is experienced in managed care contracting. A decisive individual who possesses a "big picture" perspective and is well versed in systems.

  Master's degree (MA) or equivalent; or four to ten years' related experience and/or training; or equivalent combination of education and experience.

- **Language Skills.** Ability to read, analyze, and interpret the most complex documents. Ability to respond effectively to the most sensitive inquiries or complaints. Ability to write speeches and articles in original or innovative techniques or style. Ability to make effective and persuasive speeches and presentations on controversial or complex topics to top management, public groups, and/or boards of directors.

- **Mathematical Skills.** Ability to apply advanced mathematical concepts such as exponents, logarithms, quadratic equations, and permutations. Ability to apply mathematical operations to such tasks as frequency distribution, determination of test reliability and validity analysis of variance, correlation techniques, sampling theory, and factor analysis.

- **Reasoning Ability.** Ability to apply principles of logical or scientific thinking to a wide range of intellectual and practical problems. Ability to deal with nonverbal symbolism (Formulas, scientific equations, graphs, etc.) in its most difficult phases. Ability to deal with a variety of abstract and concrete variables.

## AMERICANS WITH DISABILITY SPECIFICATIONS
## PHYSICAL DEMANDS

The physical demands described here are representative of those that must be met by an employee to successfully perform the essential functions of this job. Reasonable accommodations may be made to enable individuals with disabilities to perform the essential functions.

While performing the duties of this job, the employee is occasionally required to stand; walk; sit; use hands to finger, handle, or feel objects, tools or controls; reach with hands and arms; climb stairs; balance; stoop, kneel, crouch or crawl; talk or hear; taste or smell. The employee must occasionally lift and/or move up to 25 pounds. Specific vision abilities required by the job include close vision, distance vision, color vision, peripheral vision, depth perception, and the ability to adjust focus.

## WORK ENVIRONMENT

Work environment characteristics described here are representative of those that must be met by an employee to successfully perform the essential functions of this job. Reasonable accommodations may be made to enable individuals with disabilities to perform the essential functions.

While performing the duties of this job, the employee is exposed to weather conditions prevalent at the time.

The noise level in the work environment is usually moderate.

*Source*: "Sample Behavioral and Competency Based Job Description." Durham, NC: Duke University Human Resources (2004). Available: www.hr.duke.edu/utilities/managers/behavioral_job_description.html. (Reproduced with permission.)

# INDEX

# ABOUT THE AUTHORS

Dr. John M. Cohn and Ms. Ann L. Kelsey are Director and Associate Director respectively of the Sherman H. Masten Learning Resource Center at the County College of Morris in Randolph, New Jersey, and partners in DocuMentors, an independent consulting firm.

Previous Neal-Schuman books coauthored by Dr. Cohn, Ms. Kelsey, and Mr. Keith M. Fiels, Executive Director of the American Library Association, include *Planning for Integrated Systems and Technologies: A How-To-Do-It Manual for Librarians* (2001), *Writing and Updating Technology Plans: A Guidebook with Sample Plans on CD-ROM* (2000), and *Planning for Automation: A How-To-Do-It Manual for Librarians* (2nd ed., 1997; 1st ed., 1992).